Day Island
a glimpse of the past

Day Island
a glimpse of the past

By
Marcia Willoughby Tucker

Illustrated by
Janet Snyder Ellison

Rhododendron Press

Copyright © 1997 by Marcia E. Tucker.
Illustrations © 1997 by Janet Elison.
All rights reserved.

Library of Congress Catalogue Number: 97-91923

For Jerry

Acknowledgments

Murry Morgan's research assignments in his history classes at Tacoma Community College started me digging into Day Island's history in the 1970s. That research became the backbone of this book.

The kindness of the people who shared their recollections of Day Island's past, brought the book to life. I enjoyed interviewing: Myrtle Anderson, Alf Anderson, Bob Anderson, Mary Babare, George Babare, Jr., Doris Beattie, Gertrude Bonell, Julian Bower, Ed Bradford, Marion Brantner, my sister, Lorayne Breazeale, Eva Brown, Louise Brown, Nancy Brown, Mel and Eunice Brown, Forrest Cayton, Frederick Dean, Eugene Emmons, Henry and Agnes Foss, Elizabeth Gellerman, Neut Grimes, Frank Gropper, Henrietta Foss Hager, John Hanson, Leonard Higgins, Miriam Kelso, Bertha Kesler, Susan Knight, Lawrence Lord, Esther MacArthur, Earl Mamlock, Mel Monson, Elmer Muzzy, Stewart Nichols, Roy Norman, Harry Norman, Anna Norris, John O'Ryan, Shirley Nyman Papé, Victoria Hanson Riley, Ann Sears, Barrie Sulgrove Smith, Violet Smith, Frank and Bessie Stephens, Virginia Tanzler, Marion Todd, George Uhlman, Richard Uhlman, Marion Van Winkle, Josephine Welch, Julian Whaley, Helen Wick, Betty Wilcox, Gunneld Willits, my parents, Bill and Hazel Willoughby, my brother, Ken Willoughby, F. Bernard Wright, and Ione Wright.

Thanks are also due to: Nona Adams, Cecelia Svinth Carpenter, Roger Edwards, Corinna Goff, Gayla Goller, Danny Grecco, Hazel Heckman, Stan Marshall, Polly Medlock, Renee Paine, James Reynolds, Pam and Ross Taylor, Nile Thompson, Kay Williams, Alice Winters and Gertrude Young.

Paul Clee, photography instructor at Tacoma Community College, captured several of the early Islanders on film. Childhood friend, Pat Wilcox Flynn, spent hours typing, weeding out mistakes and designing. Another talented childhood friend, Janet Snyder Ellison, drew the illustrations.

I need to mention the librarians at the Washington State

Historical Society, including Frank Green; Jean Engerman Crisp of the Washington State Library; Gary Reese, Brian Kamens and Jean Gillmer of the Tacoma Public Library; Dr. Paul G. Spitzer, corporate historian for the Boeing Company; Georgia Franklin of the Museum of Flight; Nancy Pryor of the Washington State Library, and Elizabeth Winroth of the Oregon Historical Society.

Gary Reese and Murray Morgan read the manuscript.
My husband, Jerry, helped and encouraged.
My deepest appreciation to all.

—Marcia Tucker

Foreword

Marcia Tucker's charming study of Day Island, the humpbacked sandspit just off-shore from Tacoma in the Puget Sound Narrows, shows how good such local histories can be. Rigorously researched, written with affection but clear eyes, a respect for fact and a sense of humor, it shows why residents regard their community as "almost paradise." It describes the way a neighborhood community can, without formal organization, solve problems, as when the women of the Island formed a Garbage Brigade that not only cleaned up the beaches but tidied the Sixth Avenue approach to the Island, attracting so much attention that the City of Tacoma accepted responsibility for maintaining the neatness. This is a welcome addition to our regional literature.

—*Murray Morgan, April 1997*

Contents

Page

Chapter I
    The Early Years 1

Chapter II
    Services Rendered 15

Chapter III
    Flying Machines and Home-Grown
    Engines 29

Chapter IV
    Here's Progress 37

Chapter V
    The Willits Brothers 45

Chapter VI
    Almost Paradise 51

Chapter VII
    Through Adventures and Trials 67
    "Day Island," a poem by Frances Johnson ... 79

Notes
    Chapter I 81
    Chapter II 85
    Chapter III 87
    Chapter IV 89
    Chapter V 92
    Chapter VI 94
    Chapter VII 97

The Early Days
Chapter I

"O it's a snug little island!
A right little, tight little island"

Day Island seldom finds its way to the maps of Puget Sound. Even maps featuring the topography of the southern Sound tend to overlook it. There are reasons for this. Day Island is low-banked and small—less than a mile long, and from particular angles it blends in with the mainland shore in University Place. Both Fox Island, across the Sound to the west, and Steilacoom, a few miles to the south, see the blending effect and fail to notice the Island's slender, curving, shape. Its shape, Islanders say, resembles a sea-horse.

The sea-horse's "tail," a skinny sandspit, runs parallel with the shore and narrows to connect with the mainland at Lemon's Beach. Because of this land connection, Day Island is defined as a peninsula, but Wilkes' charts show it as an island in the early days.[1]

In the spring of 1841, Commander Charles Wilkes of the U.S. Exploring Expedition, sailed into Puget Sound aboard the flagship Vincennes. He ordered longboat crews to explore the Sound south of the Narrows. The crew presumably circled Day Island. Their detailed charts point out that a narrow passage separated the tip of the south sandspit from the mainland.[2] Frederick Dean, a Tacoma druggist who camped near the tip of the sandspit in the early 1900s recalled the Northern Pacific Railroad filled the passage in while laying tracks along the shore at Lemon's Beach.[3]

Wilkes named many locations in Puget Sound, choosing most of the names from the men of his crew. Day Island was named for Stephen W. Days, a hospital steward with the Expedition.[4] According to historian Edmond Meany, the "s" in Days was dropped in error about 85 years ago, and the Island has been known as Day Island ever since.[5]

Long-time residents doubt if Wilkes had much to do with the naming of the Island. They claim the name was given to honor the day or days of the year when high tides used to rush across the gravel at the bottom of the steep hill that overlooks the sandspit. On those days, the flood waters cut off the sandspit and created an unmistakable island. It was a time for celebrating. The boat-minded shoved off from shore in rowboats or canoes and circled the Island while their neighbors cheered them on from their vantage point on the hill. Betty Wilcox, who grew up on the Island, says, "We children joined the fun and dug trenches to encourage the flooding waters to stay awhile longer."

Rather than naming the Island as a complete entity, the Indians of Puget Sound named specific sites on the Island, as was their custom. According to historian T.T. Waterman, one

Occasionally high winter tides still storm across the land at the bottom of the south spit hill.

site was called Tse xw te, which means "itching back."[6] The exact location is not known; however, it was probably the slightly elevated strip of beach off the west shore in the center of the Island where the clams are most plentiful. Day Islanders have a similar name for it: Since the early 1900s this

A view of Crystal Creek in the 1970s near the railroad tracks at W. 19th Street. (Photo by the author)

approximately 600-foot stretch of beach has been known as "the hog's back." Waterman's other listing is Tkeba'le,[7] the word for "duck hunting place." The duck hunting season brought the Indians to the Island.

The south sandspit was a center of activity during hunting season. In the half-light of dawn or at twilight, the Indians arrived at the slender neck of land and prepared to net ducks. In a fashion that was unique to Puget Sound tribes, the Indians braced tall poles in the sandy gravel. Twelve-foot-long netting hung from a cable between the poles. The fine mesh netting was large enough for a duck to poke its head through but small enough so the bird could not pull free. Hunters in canoes startled the ducks as they slumbered in the water. When the awakened ducks attempted to fly across the sandspit to freedom, they flew into the waiting net. The hunters on the sandspit quickly released the poles and the net, bulging with their catch, collapsed on the beach where the ducks were flogged to death by the hunters' sticks.[8]

After the hunt, the Indians returned to their encampment at Crystal Creek on the mainland across the shallow lagoon from Day Island's east shore. According to Edward Huggins, a clerk at Fort Nisqually who spent a night at the Creek in March of 1852, the campsite had been in use for a long time. He wrote:

> *Just a little before dark, we reached the usual encampment, a small streamlet, on the mainland at the north end of 'Days' Island, called by the Indians 'Tukamalie,' and from the large mound of shells there, it had evidently been a camping ground for centuries.*[9]

Indians from Steilacoom and Wollochet Bay shared the encampment and hunting grounds. In the 1850s, Sam Young, headman of the Indians from Steilacoom, and the people from his village at Steilacoom Creek [Chamber's Creek], made seasonal trips to Day Island to hunt ducks. Tom White was born at Day Island on one of the hunting trips. Years later Tom's son, Clarance, was born at a camp at Sunset Beach, believed to be an intermediate stopping place between

Steilacoom and Day Island.[10]

In 1869, Anthony Roberts Williamson, a farmer in his early 30s hailing from Pennsylvania, staked a claim that included Day Island and acreage across the lagoon on the mainland. The mainland parcel of his land, about one hundred acres, was across from the southern half of Day Island and ran deep into the woods.[11] Williamson built two wooden structures on the mainland by a stream that flowed into the lagoon near the south end of his claim. One was a small house, 24 x 16 feet with a shingle roof, the other a large barn with a shed. He plowed an acre and a half of the land and built a fence. After a year, in accordance with the pre-emption act of 1841, Williamson purchased the 160.70 acres from the U.S. Government for $1.25 per acre. Then he decided to relocate.[12]

In 1871, Williamson sold his property for one thousand dollars and moved up near the Skagit River where the town of Lyman is now located. Williamson found his niche. He farmed hops and became the first settler in the Skagit Valley.[13]

Day Island's new owners, Brevet General August Valentine Kautz and his wife, Fannie, bought it as a long-term investment. Kautz, a German-born West Point graduate who grew up in Brown County, Ohio, first saw Day Island in 1853. At that time, he was a second lieutenant stationed with Company C of the Fourth Infantry at Fort Steilacoom.[14] Shortly after arriving at Fort Steilacoom, Kautz, Dr. John M. Haden, the Fort's surgeon, and Edmond Starling, the Indian agent, boarded an open launch and started up the Sound on an expedition. Kautz's diary for May 23, 1853, mentioned they stopped at Day Island for lunch. Kautz described Day Island as "a beautiful piece of land covered by an impenetrable pyramidal forest." Whether or not his diary contained other comments on Day Island will remain a mystery: it was eaten by termites.[15]

After retiring from the Army, Kautz and Fannie moved to Seattle where he died in 1895. Day Island became Fannie's responsibility. Over the next three years, as she pondered its future, campers and beachcombers from Tacoma discovered

Day Island. Among them was the late general's nephew, Dixon Kautz.

In May 1896, a year after August Kautz's death, bushy-browed, serious minded Dixon Kautz arrived in Tacoma. He peered at the hills, scanned the pewter sky and wrote to his father, George, in Moweaqua, Illinois, "It's the rottenest place I've ever struck." Kautz claimed he had yet to meet anyone who wanted to stay in Tacoma permanently. "They are all planning to make lots of money and leave, and that has left an awfully hard impression in my mind."[16]

Day Island may have helped soothe the impression, because it became his weekend retreat where he fished, read and dug a few clams. In the early days, Kautz rode out from town on the street car and hiked down the 19th Street trail to John Higgins' campground, known as Higgins Beach. He kept

Dixon Kautz is second from right.

his boat at Higgins Beach, which was the stretch of beach south of Crystal Creek. From there, he rowed across the lagoon to his cabin on the Island's east shore.[17]

A carpenter named Hubert built Kautz a comfortable one-room log cabin which had plenty of small-paned windows and a shingle roof. Kautz's ledger shows Hubert completed the cabin in November 1897. It cost $42. The price included clearing the land, splitting cedar shakes for the roof, cutting the logs, flooring, doors, windows, and the labor for

Hubert and his three assistants.[18]

While Dixon Kautz enjoyed Day Island, Fannie Kautz struggled under the burden of ownership. She owed property taxes and lacked money. In 1898, she mortgaged the Island to P.V.N. Meyers of College Hill, Ohio, for $10,000.[19] Fannie hoped to sell the property. She advertised for a buyer, and caught the attention of many speculative investors, or

Kautz's cabin. (Courtesy of Washington State Historical Society.)

so the stories tell. Over the years, Islanders have heard stories about a friend, relative or acquaintance who could have bought the little Island but thought better of it.

Stewart Nichols, a machinist, recalls a story that his father-in-law, Nathaniel Wheeler, told him: Nathaniel and his friends duck hunted on the Island in their youth. When it was advertised for sale, Nathaniel and his friends considered pooling their money to purchase the Island as a group investment, but they decided against it. Stewart is not sure why the change of heart, but it may have been the price: $300.

One Islander heard a likely buyer story during a physical examination. Her physician claimed that he heard that Julian Mamlock's son, Henry, had an opportunity to purchase the Island many years ago. Julian, a Polish immigrant who came to Tacoma in the 1890s, operated a saloon on Puyallup Avenue. One day a man sauntered into the saloon and motioned to Henry, who was working with his father. Henry approached the stranger and watched as the man reached in and pulled out a paper from his vest pocket. The paper was a property deed for Day Island, and the stranger offered it to Henry for $200. Julian, who overheard the conversation, urged his son to invest in the pint-sized island. Henry declined. What good was it? It was miles from Tacoma, and only accessible by boat.

According to Melvin Monsen of Fox Island, his father, Matthew, came close to buying the Island shortly after he moved to Tacoma in 1905. When Matthew heard the Island was for sale, he rode out from town in his horse and buggy to investigate. He stopped at the top of the Sixth Avenue hill, at the road's end, and peered down at the pint-sized Island through the trees. After some thought, he decided not to risk his money in the isolated piece of land.[20] The isolated picture was about to change with the coming of the railroads.

Tacoma's second transcontinental railroad, the Chicago, Milwaukee & St. Paul, was on the way, and for a time Tacoma thought the Union Pacific would build a terminus within the city limits. This optimism sparked an interest in land development.

Edward J. Bowes, W.A. Irwin and other California developers came north and formed the Narrows Land Company in 1906. They purchased several hundred acres and developed Regents Park, a residential area now known as part of Fircrest,[21] a few miles east of Day Island.

Eugene Church, a land developer, watched Tacoma's westward expansion with interest. A native New Yorker, Church had stepped off a train in Tacoma in August 1896.[22] His boyhood friend, Malcolm Gunston, a Tacoma realtor since 1890, encouraged Church to move west and try his hand at real estate.

Tacoma suited Church. He liked the people, the climate, and the excitement of a frontier. For five years, he worked with Joshua Peirce, investment broker, and learned the business of real estate.[23] In 1907, while managing the Suburban City Land and Water Company, a real estate venture that platted a north end addition to Steilacoom,[24] Church bought Day Island.

Church incorporated the Day Island Company, a real estate company, in August 1907.[25] He acted as president and John W. Moore served as secretary. The company had five trustees and $40,000 in capital stock. They bought the 51-acre Island for $36,000 [26] and the tidelands for $1,292.13.[27] In September, Eugene Church advertised one of his visions for the Island in the *Tacoma Daily Ledger*. The heading reads: "Elaborate Swiss chalets to be built on Day Island by prominent men of affairs."[28]

The ad stated that several of the shareholders in the Day Island Company were ready to place orders for chalets with their architects. When constructed, all the chalets would have an unobstructed view of the Sound and the Olympics, and Day Island

Eugene Church, 1909 (Courtesy of Anna Norris)

would be "the most exclusive and beautiful residential district in the west." Shareholders would be granted the privilege of selecting a lot in lieu of taking stock, and, Church wrote, this affords an opportunity to make a quick and satisfactory profit.

The public ignored Church's Swiss chalet idea, but the undaunted Church moved forward. In 1908, the Day Island Company cleared a road around the perimeter of Day Island,[29] platted the land and set up a water system. Church found the springs on the mainland where the Island's first owner, Anthony Roberts Williamson, had drawn his water. The springs were across from the hill that descends to the south sandspit, near the location of the present Day Island bridge. Church used a flume to pipe water across the lagoon to connect with wooden pipes that ran to individual lots. This system had its drawbacks. Water pressure was low and got worse when the pipes clogged up, which was often.

Early Day Islander Eva Brown used to say that you never knew what to expect when you turned on the water. Leaves and twigs that washed out in the sink were not a major concern of Eva's, but she never got used to the frogs. Frogs meant it was time to row across the lagoon to clean up the springs and make necessary repairs. Over time, this became a Sunday afternoon task shared by the men on the Island.[30]

The Day Island Company built a low-slung drawbridge that was often drenched at high tide. It had a turn out in the center where a driver could pull his horse and buggy over to let another buggy pass by. The bridge met the mainland near Crystal Creek where the trail ran up the hill, later called Nineteenth Street. While the bridge was under construction, Church's advertising read:

> *After September 5 the price on all lots on Day Island will be advanced. "Day Island" is connected with the mainland at Higgin's Beach by a drawbridge now under the course of construction, and will be reached via car line on Sixth Avenue as soon as the extension now under consideration by the city council is completed. "Day Island" will be in the center of the grand boule-*

vard system now planned to encircle the entire west end of the city and the property will be worth in two years three to four times what we are asking for it today, because it is the only piece of waterfront property between Tacoma and the mouth of the Nisqually River that the railroad does not obstruct. All lots are 60 feet deep with graded streets and a fine water system now installed. Price $600.00 per lot. Salesman on the ground. Take Steilacoom car to city limits station. The property is a twenty minute walk from there, or call Eugene Church at 10th and A St.[31]

Church built a spacious wooden-framed house on the Island near the bridge. The first floor consisted of a living room with a large fireplace and a bay window with a window seat, a kitchen and a dining room. An open stairway led upstairs to the bath and three bedrooms. The house served as a real estate office for the Day Island Company until attorney Ralph Woods and his wife, Bertha, bought it for a summer home in 1910.[32]

The Day Island Company sold 34 lots in 1908.[33] Many

Church's headquarters. In 1946, present owners Bob and Hermie Anderson purchased this home where they raised their two children, Nick and Sidney.

of the new owners bought on speculation, with plans to hold on for a few years and then resell their property at a profit. However, some of those who responded to Church's advertising became long-time Day Islanders. They were: Charlie Forler, Fred and Eva Rudow and William and Stella Gellerman.

Charlie Forler, a sturdy jovial carpet installer, originally from Minnesota, bought a lot next to Kautz's cabin. He built a small weekend cottage, dug a well and spread out the welcome mat. Friends and relatives, with tents, food, and fishing rods, gravitated to Charlie's place. Frank Forler, Charlie's brother, brought his family and his gun for hunting ducks.

Marion Todd, Charlie's niece, sighed when she recalled her duck plucking chores. "It always happened the same way. The hunters would find me and my brother, Bill, playing in the lagoon. The lagoon was beautiful in those days. There were agates to be found and the water sparkled. Bill and I spent hours swinging out over the water on a rope that Uncle Charlie had tied to a tree. We would drop in and swim back to shore time and again. When we least expected it, Father and Uncle Charlie appeared with ducks they shot on the south spit. We protested but, nevertheless, spent the afternoon plucking duck feathers. Bill and I cheered when the fam-

Marion Todd, left, by Forler's well. (Courtesy of Marion Todd)

ily decided to fish or dig clams for dinner."

As the years passed, Charlie spent more time on the Island. In the 1930s, he enlarged his cottage and moved in year-round. He worked close to home in later years. He operated Titlow Beach Store, a small confectionery and gas station over at Titlow Beach.[34]

The lot Fred and Eva Rudow purchased looked west to Fox Island and beyond to the Olympics. Fred, the foreman at Allen & Lamborn Printing Company in Tacoma, built a small one-story house on his lot. By 1916 he and Eva had sold their home on North J Street and had moved permanently to Day Island.

Fred captured the title of the Island's best fisherman; no one could out-fish Fred. Eva also acquired honorable status. She cooked like a chef, excelled at bridge, and according to her neighbor, Mary Babare, Eva always finished hanging out the wash on Monday morning before the rest of the women had cleared away the breakfast dishes. The Island felt the shock in 1924 when Fred died of a heart attack while out fishing. A few months later, Eva sold the house and moved to an apartment in Tacoma.[35]

William Gellerman, the owner of Gellerman's Grocery on South Tacoma Avenue, and his wife, Estelle (Stella), selected two lots on the west side not far from the hill that leads to the south spit. After two summers of camping amongst the madrona trees, the Gellermans built a small summer house with a porch across the front.

They enclosed the porch in 1934, added a fireplace, and Will, Stella and their children, Bill Jr. and Elizabeth, moved in year-round. They remained on the Island until 1958 when they joined Bill Jr. and Beth who were living and teaching school in Concord, California.

Susan Brown Knight, who grew up across the street from the Gellermans, remembers climbing up on Will's knee to hear about all the gold Will dug during the gold rush in the Klondike. Will had worked for Gus Wagner on Eldorado Creek for over a year and came away with enough gold to marry Stella and open up his own grocery store. It was a story Will liked to retell, and Susan was a captive audience.[36]

Islanders remember Stella and her beautiful flower gardens. One of her favorite flowers was a coral spider dahlia with a yellow throat. She shared the bulbs with her neighbors, and over the years the flower became known as the "Day Island Dahlia." In the summertime it can still be found blooming in gardens along West Boulevard—a reminder of the early days on Day Island.

Services Rendered
Chapter II

Stephens' Store

In 1908, Francis Marion Stephens, the kindly proprietor of Stephens Grocery Store in Regents Park, bought several acres of land from lanky Andrew J. Littlejohn, an undertaker and land developer from Indiana. The property, which Littlejohn called the Belmarlow Addition, ran along what is now 19th Street and included Crystal Creek, where the Indians had camped.

Francis left his soft-spoken son, Frank, managing the store in Regents Park, and set out for Crystal Creek to begin a new venture. He pitched a tent on the bank of the Creek and stocked it with bread and milk and camping necessities to sell to the jovial mix of summer people who traipsed down

Littlejohn's real estate office (Photo by author, 1997)

the hill on their way to the Island. Francis enjoyed his light-hearted customers. As they grew in number and their needs increased, Francis added a storage shed and stocked more goods. He built a cluster of rental cabins next to the tent, and he and his wife, Anna Marie, lived in one of the cabins during the summer months.

Francis watched with interest as activity increased at both ends of the Day Island bridge. Over on the Island, new houses dotted the shoreline. Two of the houses belonged to the first year-round residents. Milo D. Stewart, a boatbuilder, and his wife, Mary, built on East Boulevard near Charlie Forler's place. Neva and William D. Tucker, manager of Northwestern Grocery Company, constructed a one-story house with a basement next door to Ralph Wood's summer home.[1] The Stewart's were living in their home by 1911, the Tuckers moved to the Island in 1912.[2]

A mill sprang up on the mainland shore off the north side of the bridge. Snyder Brothers Mill was the effort of lumbermen Ed and John Snyder. (After reorganizing in 1916, the name was changed to Clear Fir Lumber Company.)[3]

New growth and development inspired Francis Stephens. He decided to close the store in Regents Park and give year-round attention to Stephens' Grocery by Crystal Creek. He built on to the storage shed and ended up with a

Clear Fir Lumber Company (Courtesy of Stan Marshall)

Day Island bridge as seen from Clear Fir Lumber Company (Courtesy of Stan Marshall)

Francis Marion Stephens stands in front of his store in 1911. (Courtesy of Miriam Kelso)

respectable-looking wood framed building. Francis stocked everything from hay and kerosene to candy and cookies by the pound. He had a cheese wheel, a pickle barrel and a barrel full of vinegar. People brought in their own jug for a refill. Francis never locked the store. If the Stephens were away, the customers helped themselves and left a note, promising to pay for their purchases on their next visit.

Frank often crossed to the Island 6 or 7 times a day delivering customers' groceries. He hand-carried small orders or

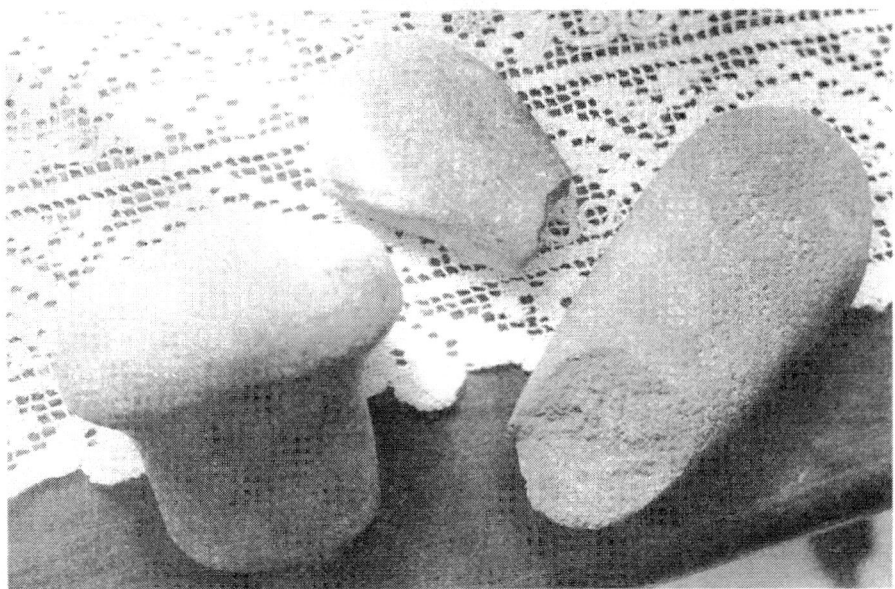

Top right, Bessie Stephens demonstrates how to use an Indian pestle. Above photo shows Indian artifacts found by Bessie in lagoon behind their home. (Photos by Paul Clee)

transported them on his bicycle. He delivered large orders in a horse-drawn wagon. After he purchased a Model T Ford and attached a wooden carrier to the back, deliveries were easier and quicker, giving Frank more time to work on engines. Soon after the store became a year-round business in 1912, a garage was added and later a gas station, which Frank managed.

In 1914, after a five-year courtship, Frank married Bessie Thompson of Regents Park. For a year, the young couple rented a house on the Island and then built a cottage on East Boulevard where the entrance to the bridge is presently located. After Francis retired, Bessie managed Stephens' Grocery while Frank worked in the garage. The Stephens' daughters, Miriam and Jeanne, helped out part-time. By the mid-'40s business slowed to a trickle. Bessie established a career in real estate, and the store became Frank's charge. He kept the "free" candy jar full for the children who stopped by. Frank and his young friends liked to gather around the pot belly stove and swap stories. In the 1960s, Frank closed the doors for the last time, but he and Bessie stayed close by. They spent the rest of their days living behind the old store in cabins that Francis Stephens had built years before.[4]

Lemon's Beach and the Milk Wagon

The farm, which had once been home to Nancy Weston and her husband, Rodolphus, stretched out across from the Island's south sandspit. Rodolphus, a blacksmith and Baptist minister from Connecticut, staked his claim in 1895. According to Bonney's History of Pierce County, Rodolphus conducted several of the early marriages in the County. In 1889, the Westons sold the farm to John and Mary Lemon and moved to Steilacoom.[5]

John Lemon, a Civil War veteran from Ohio, improved and promoted the farm. He advertised for weekenders to come to Lemon's Beach and rent a camping space or one of his newly-built cabins. He cultivated orchards of apples, cherries and pears and grew a variety of berries. When the Northern Pacific Railroad asked permission to feature his farm in advertising pamphlets, he was pleased. However, when he heard the N.P. planned to run a shore route from Steilacoom to Tacoma through his property, Lemon's mood soured.

According to his obituary notice, when surveyors showed up and ran lines across his land and drove stakes in his orchards,

Top photo, John Lemon (Photo courtesy of Wheelock Collection, Tacoma Public Library). Lower photo, Northern Pacific Railroad footbridge.

"the ire of the veteran was aroused." After months of negotiating, Lemon received a $25,000 settlement for a strip of land 160 feet wide and about 1,200 feet long. In failing health, Lemon put the farm up for rent, and he and Mary moved to Tacoma.[6] Lemon died before the first train rounded the bend at Lemon's Beach in 1914, so he missed seeing the new timber footbridge that straddled the tracks where fruit trees once bloomed. He also missed hearing about the adventures the children from the Island experienced atop the N.P.'s 107-foot-long footbridge.[7]

Islander Marian Van Winkle recalls that the footbridge was a delightful place to play. The children ran up one staircase, darted across the top and raced down the stairs on the opposite side. The boys hung by their hands and dangled over the tracks. According to Frederick Dean who camped with his wife, Alice, near the footbridge and witnessed the children's play, "No harm was done. The children built memories, and all lived to tell about it." The N.P. dismantled the footbridge in 1923, much to the chagrin of the children.

Nels Johansen, a fisherman, and his wife, Ida, rented the Lemon's farm from 1913 to 1919. During the summer months, Nels fished in Alaska, leaving Ida at home to care for their children, Emil and Myrtle.

To help pass the time while Nels was away, Ida came up with a profitable plan to entertain the children. They started a milk route to Day Island. Ida milked the cows and filled quart bottles. In the late afternoon or early evening, depending on the tide, the children hitched up their pony to a one-seat Studebaker cart, loaded the milk into an open box that rested behind the seat and started out. Myrtle says the bottles clattered together as they made their way along the skinny sandspit and climbed the hill. The children circled the Island, pausing at each camping site, eager to sell to new campers as well as their regular customers.

Myrtle remembers the diversity of the Island houses. There were the year-round houses, designed to last—many were two-story, and tent houses, made of canvas stretched over a wooden frame and secured to a base. Some families built summer homes that grew over time. Rooms for sleeping and storage were tacked on, sun porches closed in, kitchens enlarged. Often the walls were out-of-square and the floors sloped, but no one seemed to mind. What mattered was extra space.

Myrtle noted that one of the lots on the west beach held two two-story houses.[8] Charles and Mathilda Williams shared the lot that they purchased in 1913 with their daughter Alma and her husband, Gustave (Gus) Nyman. They dug a well.

Day Island tent house (Courtesy of Marion Todd)

The Nymans, who had a daughter, Shirley, moved to the Island year-round in 1919. In 1925, the Williams moved into a smaller house which they squeezed onto the north side of the property.[9]

Myrtle enjoyed watching the Island grow and change during the years she and Emil delivered milk to the Island. When she grew up, she married Albin Anderson and lived nearby on Sunset Drive in University Place.

The Butcher Boat

Frederick Dean remembers that Day Islanders looked forward to shopping aboard Richard Uhlman's floating market. Richard brought his boat, "The Butcher," ashore at the north end of the sandspit, and by the time he laid out the gangplank, his customers were on hand ready to shop. The stock aboard included meat from Uhlman's Meat Market in Old Tacoma, canned goods and camping supplies.

"The Butcher," built by Crawford and Reed Shipyard, had a nine-foot beam and a 14-horse power Hallin engine. According to Richard Jr., his dad ran "The Butcher" on the Sound for about six years, and Day Island was one of the regular stops. When small stores began cropping up along the Sound, business dropped off and Richard closed his market in Old Town and opened up a store at Wollochet Bay. He sold "The Butcher" around 1914.[10] By then the Islanders scanned the Sound, watching for Oscar Gustovensen's boat to cross over from Fox Island.

The Egg Man

Oscar Gustovensen, Day Island's Finnish egg man, first pulled his boat up on the beach around 1913. Gussie rowed over from his Fox Island farm once or twice a week, often accompanied by his lively daughter, Haydee. He journeyed across all year round. Neither storms nor cold temperatures kept Gussie home.

When Gussie's customers saw him landing, they hurried down to the beach and filled their egg bowls from his wicker baskets before he began his rounds. He used a wheelbarrow to transport the eggs, and sometimes chickens and winter apples, around the Island. Gussie fed his hens milk, which resulted in high quality eggs. According to Roy Norman and other Islanders, the eggs surpassed any they ever tasted. For over 30 years, Islanders applauded Gussie as he faithfully rowed the eggs across the Sound.[11]

The Yellowhammer

Shortly after Gussie began his delivery service, Newton Muzzy saw a way to earn a living on the Island. Muzzy, a jitney driver on 6th Avenue, drove a Reo, a 1910 five-passenger touring car. Sixth Avenue was alive with jitney drivers by 1914, and Muzzy desired a change from the hectic pace. After a road was cut through attorney Aaron Titlow's property, Muzzy noted the increase in the number of people requiring transportation out to Day Island and decided to start a bus route.[12]

A road through Titlow's land had been slow in coming. In 1911, Titlow built a three-story Swiss chalet style hotel, the Hotel Hesperides. His property, which was the northern half of the William B. Wilton donation land claim, included most of the land at the west end of 6th Avenue. He laid a planked road that met with 6th Avenue and wound down the hill past the hotel to the beach. Day Islanders asked Titlow to extend the road another 1,600 feet to connect with 19th Street but, as a 1910 newspaper article states, Titlow had no interest in cutting through to 19th Street. However, he agreed to dedicate property for Day Islanders and other interested parties to build a road at their expense. Nothing happened until the city stepped in. By 1914 Titlow's land was annexed to Tacoma, and the city replaced the planked road with a paved surface and extended it to 19th Street.[13]

Muzzy started a bus route.

Muzzy bought a three-quarter ton GMC 1915 model truck and built a body on it. It held 16 buckboard-type seats and had isinglass windows with side curtains. Muzzy painted his bus a sunny yellow and named it the Yellowhammer, after the Northern Flicker. He found a bird-like whistle, and as the Yellowhammer rumbled across the bridge and circled the Island, the whistle sang out, announcing the bus's arrival.

Muzzy made continual stops on the Island, collecting

passengers and picking up lists of errands which he tended to between bus runs. He mailed packages and shopped. Muzzy transported anything that he could squeeze into the Yellowhammer, including furniture, stoves and washing machines. Eva Brown said, "Mr. Muzzy was a perfect gentleman. He always got off the bus and carried my parcels down to our house."

The indispensable bus service blossomed. In 1916, Muzzy added two more buses to the route. He called one bus "the Bluebird"; the second was another Yellowhammer. The Bluebird held 30 people and used to be a jitney that ran up to Mt. Rainier. It was stubby and low, with no room for standing.

It caught the attention of the boys on the Island. The boys tied a rope to a tree that grew on top of the bank on East Boulevard, not far from the bridge. As the Bluebird passed by, the children swung out over the bus and dropped on the top for a free ride. Leonard Higgins, who spent summers on the Island, said, "I was the only kid who could sail out over the bus one-handed. I was also the only one who fell and broke an arm." Muzzy's 18-year-old son, Elmer, drove the second Yellowhammer. The buses left from 9th and Broadway; round-trip cost 25 cents.

Elmer recalls stopping at the Hotel Hesperides while the Islanders disembarked to pick up their mail at the post office. He claims the buses made seven trips a day to the Island, starting at 7 a.m., which was the men's work bus. The last run was at 10 p.m. The bus business showed a profit, but Elmer says that when his parents divorced in 1918, his Dad traded the buses for a farm on Vashon Island. Day Islanders missed the Muzzys and their personalized service.

Gropper

German-born Fred Gropper started knocking on doors looking for work about the same time that Muzzy began his bus route. "Is your master at home?" Gropper inquired when a homemaker peered out the door, for the shaggy handyman in his wide-brimmed hat and hip boots preferred doing business with the man of the house. To him women meant trouble. According to Gropper, they caused all the stopped-up sinks and clogged septic tanks on the Island. Gropper occasionally interrupted a gathering of the women long enough to voice his opinion and scold them for their careless ways. Although he was stubborn and annoying at times, most of the women disregarded Gropper's peculiarities and claimed that he was a good man who worked hard to support his large family.

The Groppers lived at Sunset Beach, south of Lemon's Beach. Gropper sighted the stretch of beach during the summer of 1913 while driving steel for the N.P.'s Steilacoom to Tacoma route. He hurried home to Midland, Wash., and returned with his family. He had met his wife, Mary, a former school teacher, in South Dakota. The Groppers had seven children who were ten years old and younger when they moved to Sunset Beach.

Gropper claimed squatters' rights on five acres, where the land comes to a point. His family camped in an abandoned shack while Gropper and his eldest son, Frank, salvaged lumber off the beach. Gropper constructed a six-room house and topped it off with a gabled roof. He added an oversized stone fireplace and installed a wood furnace. When the job with the N.P. ended, Gropper worked on the Island full time. He stayed for more than 30 years, tackling any job that came his way. Gropper chopped down trees and built stone fireplaces and chimneys; some are still in use. He stacked driftwood and assembled bulkheads to prevent the land from sliding into the Sound. He dug basements.

Frank Gropper quit school at age 16 and for a time worked alongside his father. Frank recalls that while digging a basement at the Taylor's house, which was on the west side, north of the "hog's back," he and his father uncovered two skeletons, and surmised they were Indian remains. Frank does not recall what became of the skeletons. On two other occasions, graves were unearthed near the first site.[14]

Gropper ended up divorced and living in one of the hobo shacks across the lagoon. In the 1950s, the Day Island

Yacht Club bought the property where the shacks stood. They ordered all trespassers off their land. All left peacefully, except Gropper, who lingered until after he had a court hearing — with Judge Burtil Johnson. "I'm gonna take that Swede judge's advice and get out," Gropper told the *Tacoma News Tribune*. Gropper, with steel-rimmed spectacles perched on his upturned nose, said that before the sheriff got there to evict him on Monday (Dec. 20, 1954), he'd be on a train headed for Nebraska to visit relatives for Christmas. Gropper pointed to a sign on a nearby madrona tree that read:

**Private Property
Day Island Yacht Club
Members and Guests Only.**

Gropper winked slyly. He outlasted the other squatters, now he must move on. Gropper packed his suitcase the following Monday but held up inside as Lester Magaw from the Day Island Yacht Club set fire to his shack. Gropper lasted until the smoke drove him out, then he grabbed his suitcase and headed down the railroad tracks, which he had helped lay many years before.[15]

Stories about Gropper, Muzzy and the others who provided services for Day Islanders in the early days continue to live on in the hearts of those who remember.

Titlow Beach-Day Island Stage. Thomas Henry Whitman with wife Emily and children. The driver, Fred Stover, far right. (Courtesy of Washington State Historical Society.)

Flying Machines and Home-grown Engines
Chapter III

Before they built their own place in 1918, Jesse and Eva Brown and their young daughter, Reba, spent two summers tenting alongside Elmo and Betty Brown's cottage. Elmo, Jesse's brother, worked at the Tacoma Tribune as a printer. Jesse was a photo engraver for Tacoma Engraving Company. The men rode together to and from work aboard Muzzy's Yellowhammer bus and both, Eva Brown says, were dependable, hard-working men.

Neither of them resembled Stromer, the free spirit who rented John Graham's house on the south spit hill (2256 Day Island Blvd. W.), and Eva hoped the brothers would not become tainted by their frequent conversations with the foreigner, who spoke with a thick accent, and said Eva, had the look of a spy.[1]

In 1900, at age 15, Gustave Waldemar Stromer from Helsingborg, Sweden, arrived in New York aboard the vessel, "Norge."[2] Little is known about his early years in America, however, a newspaper article mentioned that by the time he was 16, Stromer was "actively interested in the construction of flying machines."[3]

By 1912, the brawny, brown-eyed adventurer was building and flight testing aeroplanes at his home and shop in South Tacoma.[4] During one flight, while circling at about 60 feet, Stromer lost control of his bi-plane and crash landed. He crawled out of the wreckage, bruised, but more calm than any of the onlookers, eager to begin repairing the damages. "Accidents will happen," said Stromer. "I'll have this bi-plane working again in 2 or 3 days. Nothing to it."[5]

Stromer's determination and thirst for adventure accompanied him when he moved to Day Island. In an area that was later closed in for a basement, he set up a shop where he designed and built flying machines, machine parts, and accessories. He tested one of his inventions, a metal cone-shaped bomb-dropping device, while flying over the Narrows at an altitude of around 1,000 feet. Near Salmon Beach, Stromer aimed at a predetermined target and released the

Believed to be Conrad Hanson.

Stromer standing on his hydroaeroplane near Point Defiance.

wires on his device. A crowd of spectators watched from the shore as an imitation bomb plunged toward the water.[6] Conrad Hanson, Stromer's assistant and business manager, reported to the press that the device could drop up to eight bombs at a time.[7]

The first Island-built flying machine, a 16-foot long hydroaeroplane had a spruce body and parallel wings. The top wing was 43 feet, the lower one, 31 feet. Stromer powered the machine with an 80-horse power Curtiss engine and guided it with his feet.[8]

Frank Stephens, a small investor in the plane venture, recalls that on weekends people gathered on the beach, eager for a chance to soar above the Sound with birdman Stromer. Most paid a fee, but a few, like Charles Roediger, were complimentary fliers. Roediger, a newspaper reporter and photographer, carried a camera with him and shot some of the first aerial views of the Sound.[9] Another complimentary flier, Ione Titlow Wright, said her flight was the thrill of a lifetime.

Ione met Stromer aboard the Yellowhammer. "The bus broke down at the top of Titlow hill, and there I was loaded down with packages. Stromer saw my predicament, introduced himself and offered to carry my packages," said Ione. "While strolling down the hill, he asked me over for a ride in his flying machine the following Sunday. I accepted. It was a wonderful experience. We nose-dived and loop-de-looped. We made a date to fly to Olympia, and I mistakenly told my father."

Ione recalled, "My father's (Aaron Titlow) eyes narrowed as he peered over the rim of his spectacles." He said, "No decent woman ever rode in a flying machine." The ride was very noisy—nothing much could happen up there, but Father's word was law. In those days one had to keep oneself marriageable, so I stayed away from flying machines and never saw Stromer again."[10]

During the time Stromer lived on the Island, "The Stromer Company" kept an office in the Berlin Building at 11th and Pacific where the Washington Building now stands. The city directory lists T. Oliver MacDonald, a broker from

Milton, as company president and Stromer as vice president. If MacDonald contributed funds to Stromer's venture, it failed to ease the cash flow problems. Frank Stephens said Stromer was always broke. Fees earned from his aerial tours helped pay the rent but in order to continue with his experiments, Stromer needed to generate more income. One money-making scheme involved Stromer, Tacoma's mayor A.V. Fawcett, an actress and a Maxwell racing car.

Stromer opened up an air passenger service between Tacoma and Seattle. The introductory flight occurred on February 20, 1915. Jane O'Roark, a thrill-seeking actress who performed at the Empress Theater on Pacific Avenue accompanied Stromer. Jane boarded the hydroaeroplane at the city waterway, carrying two messages and a small bundle of letters, which was the first airborne mail to leave Tacoma. One of the messages, addressed to Seattle's mayor Hiram Gill, came from Mayor Fawcett. The mayor wrote: "The presentation to you of this letter by Miss Jane O'Roark will signalize the success in the latest step in the evolution of transportation between Tacoma and Seattle...." The second note was from postmaster F.L. Stocking to postmaster Edgar Battle of Seattle.

Jack Haswell, manager of the Tacoma Car Company, added a twist to the event. Haswell bet $100 that he could reach Seattle before Stromer. As the birdman lifted off from the city waterway, Haswell, in front of the Post Office, slid behind the wheel of his red Maxwell and streaked down Pacific Highway bound for Seattle. It took him 50 minutes, and according to the *Tacoma Tribune*, he won the race. However, the *Seattle PI* and the *Ledger* gave the honor to Stromer. The *Ledger* reported the flight took 27 minutes with a de layed landing due to boat traffic and choppy water.

Jane delivered the mail to the Post Office and Mayor Gill's office at city hall before driving back to Tacoma with Haswell in the Maxwell. Stromer rested up in West Seattle, then gave a ride home to Arthur Arnson, a painter, for whom he was building a plane. [11]

Success shone in Stromer's eyes. He proved his machine was reliable, and showed he could fly the distance between the two cities. "This is nothing compared to what I can do," boasted Stromer, and he set out to try and prove it.

Stromer built a 12-seat passenger plane with 100-foot wing span. He planned to power it with two 120-horsepower engines,[12] but could not raise enough money. In 1916, Stromer moved to Portland in pursuit of his dreams, but after a few more flying machine ventures, he gave up and went into the cabinet making business. Stromer disappeared from the Portland city directory in 1924, and was not heard of again. However, Day Islanders had not forgotten him.

Frederick Dean remembered that the birdman spoke with a thick accent and dropped bombs above the Sound during the First World War. Dean said, "He had the markings of a foreign spy." Eva Brown agreed.

Ben and Olga Norman's sons, Roy and Harry, were ages 7 and 8 when Stromer moved away. They recall that Stromer had a short fuse. "When he spotted curious children inching up next to his flying machine, he'd let out a yell that sent us racing for home," said Roy. Frank Stephens claims that Stromer was a genius who had no time for neighborhood children or a family of his own. "He spent all his time experimenting and dreaming up his next venture." Frank added, "With more financial backing, there's no telling what the birdman might have accomplished." Stromer would have agreed.

Carl and Louise Hallin, Swedish-born Methodists, moved to the Island about the same time as Stromer. Hallin, who learned mechanics as a boy working at his father's workshop in Skininge, Sweden, brought Louise to Tacoma by way of Denver, Colorado in the late 1890s. Hallin opened up a bicycle shop on Tacoma Avenue where he built, sold and repaired bicycles.[13] He specialized in a model he called, "the Tacoma." An advertisement in the 1903 city directory reads: "Patronize Home Industry. Ride a 'Tacoma' bicycle...best repair shop in the city."

By 1905 Hallin had closed the bicycle shop and was building gasoline powered marine engines at his home on South Trafton. One of his early works, a 70-horsepower engine, powered "the Viking," a passenger boat that ran between Tacoma and Fox Island.

Hallin relocated on the tideflats in the spring of 1910 and hired young F. Bernard (Barney) Wright as an apprentice. Barney worked on the other engines that came into the shop but said he never laid hands on a Hallin-built engine. Hallin insisted on repairing his own machines. Barney opened up "Wright Repair Company" and went into business for himself when Hallin moved Louise, their daughter, Ruth, and his business to Day Island in 1915. [14]

The Hallins built a shake house which had a basement and a wide front porch across the front (1945 Day Island Blvd. E.). A widow's walk upstairs over the porch offered a view of the Narrows. The house sat next to the bridge, about 60 feet from "Hallin's Gas Engine and Boat Company," which balanced on pilings in the lagoon.

The entrance to Hallin's Shop lined up with the bridge, allowing Hallin's customers to drive inside to conduct their business. Others came by boat and loaded their motors off the dock. The boating customers paid homage to the tide. At low tide the water drained out of the lagoon, exposing a rocky, muddy bottom which could hold an unaware boater captive

Hallin's Gas Engine & Boat Company (Courtesy of Marion Todd)

for hours.[15]

Hallin took Louis Brown in as a partner in 1919. A few years later, Louis and his warm-hearted wife, Louise, moved up the street from the Hallins. "The partnership had a short life span," said Louise. "The two worked better independently." Louis ended up renting space from Hallin, building "Brown" engines and repairing Hallin's overload. Hallin concentrated on his own 2-cycle, heavy-duty engines.[16]

According to Roy and Harry Norman, Hallin fractured his leg when a crank case caught fire and blew up after he primed it with ether. From then on, he walked with a limp.

In 1944 Hallin died at age 75,[17] and Louise sold the house to Valentine and Eva Heuertz and moved into Tacoma.[18] Although Hallin was gone, his home-grown engines continued to power boats on the Sound for many more years. One of his engines ended up in Barney Wright's marine museum—a tribute to a man who had lived and worked on Day Island.

Here's Progress
Chapter IV

Many Day Islanders purchased utility poles and hooked up to electricity when City Light ran a line across the bridge via 19th Street.[1] Along with the warmth of new lights came a desire to revitalize the Island. By 1914 the weather-beaten bridge threatened to collapse, the road was rutted and pocked with holes, and the inadequate water system, coupled with the fear of a devastating fire, were concerns that swept back and forth across the Island like the ebb and flow of the tide. A dozen of the men met together to discuss the problems, and thus began the Day Island Club.

The newly-formed club elected William Tucker, one of the first year-round residents for president. A.U. Mills, a mustached, balding, building contractor, was vice president.[2] Mills, a native New Yorker and former Pierce County Sheriff, had lived in Tacoma since the 1880s.[3] He and his wife, Margaret, migrated to the Island each year early in March. Their two-story framed house overlooked the "hog's back" and stood next door to Elmo and Betty Brown's cottage.

Fred Rudow, the "best" of the fishermen, agreed to the office of Day Island Club treasurer. Jim Garvin, a light-complexioned Tacoma businessman, signed on as secretary. He and his wife, Zelma, owned a two-story summer home that sat up the hill from the bridge. One of Gropper's fieldstone chimneys adorned the south side of the Garvin house, and a stone wall barricaded the yard from the road. Jim was the treasurer of Commercial Truck and Storage Company. The Garvins had two daughters, Jane and Ruth Ellen.[4]

A few houses north of the Garvin's place, at the foot of the north hill, was the Olson's summer home where Ben and Marie and their daughter, Evelyn, spent at least six months of the year. Olson, who owned and operated a plumbing

Zelma Garvin with daughters Jane and Ruth Ellen. (Courtesy of Gertrude Bonnell)

Men of the Island clear road to the beach. (Courtesy of Virginia Tanzler)

business (O. Ben Olson Company), served as the club's trustee.[5]

The men incorporated the Day Island Club in 1915. According to the bylaws, the club elected officers each year at the annual meeting, which met on the first Tuesday after the first Monday in October. The club collected a $1 initiation fee from its members, quarterly dues were $1. Anyone could join, but non-property owners, referred to as "social members" could not vote or hold an office.

The corporation papers show that plans were underway to establish a social club to foster and maintain athletic activities and social gatherings, and establish reading rooms, and libraries. The papers state that the club could acquire land, pipelines, franchises, etc., to supply its members with water, and could oil, pave or otherwise improve the Island's roads.[6]

Although the men of the club cleared a road down to the beach at the stub of South 19th Street in 1915, most of their "road work" required more wit than muscle. They aimed to convince the County commissioners to allocate funds to repair the bridge and road. For a number of years requests for a smoother road remained on hold, but the County did replace the low-slung bridge in 1916 with a higher, wider span. Like the original bridge, it joined the mainland shore west of the railroad tracks.[7]

The club forged ahead with other projects, both large and small. In 1917 the spirit of patriotism that swept across the nation reached the Island's shore in time for the Fourth of July. The club responded. The women bought an American flag and planned a celebration; the men erected a flag pole at the top of the north end hill. With tasks behind them, the Islanders gathered around the pole and raised Old Glory with heartfelt pride for their country and their community effort.[8] The flag sailed in the breeze for many years.

By 1918, the time had come to dig a well and establish an independent water system. The Island would no longer be at the mercy of Dr. Ernest Fisher, a dentist who owned the land where its water supply originated,[9] or Eugene Church, owner of the pipeline. Improved water pressure would be an ally in the event of a fire, and an end would come to twigs and frogs washing out in the sinks.

Mills got permission from the County to use the stub of 22nd street on East Boulevard for a well site.[10] Eugene Church agreed to sell his pipeline, including the water main across the lagoon and his franchise for $1,000.[11] Ben Olson and John Draper got bids on putting down a well and installing a pneumatic water system.[12] The club secured financing by soliciting subscriptions from the property owners. An appointed committee supervised the project. Committee members included: Mills, Draper, Ray Gillispie, an electrician, Dr. J.R. Brown and Frank Kepner, who was the first principal of Jason Lee Intermediate School. Kepner agreed to take on the job of water superintendent, a position he held for over 12 years.

Records show that Fred Gropper and Elmo Brown hired on to work alongside W.R. Wemoth, the well contractor. To increase the water pressure, the men built a 50-foot tower. They placed a water storage tank on the top. A pump was

Caroll Waldow and his dog on East Boulevard. (Courtesy of Marion Todd)

West Boulevard

installed, and during August they shut off the connection to Fisher's property, and turned on the pump.

"What a disaster!" chuckled Eva Brown. "Most of the time the water tasted salty from the high tides that seeped into the well....The water was hard, the water pressure low. The women's Monday wash looked as grey as a winter sky and felt like sandpaper next to our skin." The Club vowed to improve their independent water system as more people joined and paid their dues. (The club boosted the membership fee from $50 to $100 in January 1919.)

The Islanders constructed a small building beneath the water tower. They planned to partition off the inside for club rooms, but instead, the building, known as the pump house, became a catch-all for old water pipes, etc. Plans for a club house remained on the drawing board awaiting funding. [13]

In 1918, Henry and Agnes Foss, two Tacoma natives and graduates of Tacoma (Stadium) High School, moved to the Island. According to Henry, he and Agnes paid $5000 for George and Harriet Marvin's house on West Boulevard.

George and Harriet Marvin moved up the street in the center of the Island where there was room for a backyard tennis court. The Marvin's daughter, Virginia Tanzler, recalls that tennis became a neighborhood pastime. "My dad organized tournaments for tennis players of all ages. We invited the Islanders to play as often as they wanted." (The Islanders enjoyed the courts until the mid '50s.)[14]

The Fosses were accustomed to having the Sound at

Roy Norman at the tennis court.

their door. Their former residence, an abandoned cookhouse, stood on the water at 4th and Dock Street, next to Foss Launch & Tug Company, Henry's family's business. Henry served as company secretary and later as president.

Henry and Agnes' new two-story house had plenty of room for their growing family. Their son, Drew, was born shortly after they moved to the Island; their daughter, Henrietta (Tooty), was born a few years later. The Fosses painted the exterior of their house green and white, official Foss Company colors.[15]

Soon after he moved to the Island, Henry joined the road improvement committee. He met with the commissioners of public works and reported back to the Club at the October 1919 meeting that the County had appropriated funds for paving the road in the 1920 budget. The Islanders rejoiced as they looked forward to driving on smoother roads.

George and Mary (Tomich) Babare, natives of (Austra-Hungary) Yugoslavia, had been married for five years in the fall of 1919 when they took a scenic ride out to Day Island.

"We were driving along when we spotted a 'for sale'

sign that realtor (G.D.) Grant had nailed up on a two-story house on West Boulevard. It was love at first sight." Mary added that the house belonged to A.U. Mills. The Babares bought their dream house and soon moved in with their three-year-old son, George Jr. Their second son, Bob, was born in 1921.

George owned and operated "Babare Boat Building" with his younger brother, Nick. The brothers had learned boatbuilding from their father, Stefan Babare, who built ships in Old Tacoma in the late 1890s. George and Nick, specialists in deep-sea fishing boats, opened their business in Old Tacoma, but relocated to the Hylebos Waterway in 1919.[16]

Mary said she would never forget George's first community effort after they moved to the Island. One Sunday morning in 1920, some of the men, Oliver Craig, Gus Nyman, George Marvin and her George, met on the hill, up from the bridge, to erect a flag pole next to Dr. Elizabeth Drake's house. "It was a battle of wills. They all assumed the role of foreman, arguing over the flag's location, the strength of the pulley, etc.," chuckled Mary, her hazel eyes laughing. The new flag pole replaced the original community flag pole which was removed to make way for the paving of the road.

Ben and Olga Norman's sons, Roy and Harry, tagged along as the road crew

Henry Foss (Courtesy of Henry Foss, 1978)

43

began their work. Harry recalls that a team of horses dragged a two-handled Colorado scraper around the Island, scooping off the ruts and filling in the low spots. A scow loaded with sand and gravel anchored off the north side of the bridge, at the deepest part of the channel. On board, the workmen built a hopper and mixed up the cement. After they poured the cement and smoothed out the surface, the road crew began working its way up the hill. They resurfaced all of Day Island-Regents Park Boulevard, which curved past University Place School (where most of the Island children attended classes) and ran all the way to Fircrest (Grandview to 27th Street). After the road crew departed, Harry and Roy christened the road by scratching their initials in the fresh cement.[17]

With smooth roads at their doorsteps and a water system to call their own, the Islanders looked forward to the challenges of the future.

The Willits Brothers
Chapter V

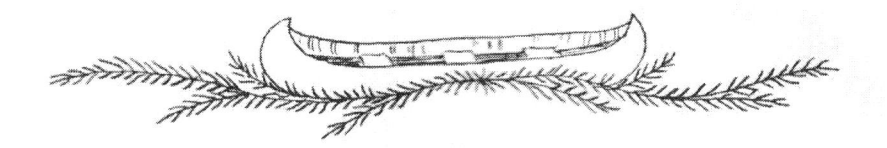

In 1905, two boys, Earl C. and Floyd C. Willits, accidentally stumbled across their life's work at their home in Des Moines, Iowa—they built a canoe.[1] The Willits family migrated to Tacoma a few years later. Earl, a serious-minded high school student, and his brother, Dwight, a carpenter, moved first.[2] On their heels came Floyd, the light-hearted youngest brother, their sister, Ruth, and their widowed father, Clinton H. Willits, a building contractor.[3]

Earl and Floyd experimented with different canoe designs in their back yard while attending Tacoma (Stadium) High School. Following Floyd's high school graduation in 1913, the boys opened up a small shop on Wollochet Bay,

Floyd and Earl Willits. (All Willits photos courtesy of Gunneld Willits)

which, they boasted, "was the first canoe manufacturing plant west of Chicago."[4]

They closed their shop during World War I and enlisted in the military—Earl served in the Air Force, Floyd joined the Army. After the War, the brothers returned home and built one canoe after another, improving the Ardendale river canoe design to increase its stability in coastal waters. They also made the decision to relocate on Day Island, a place where they had picnicked during their high school days.[5]

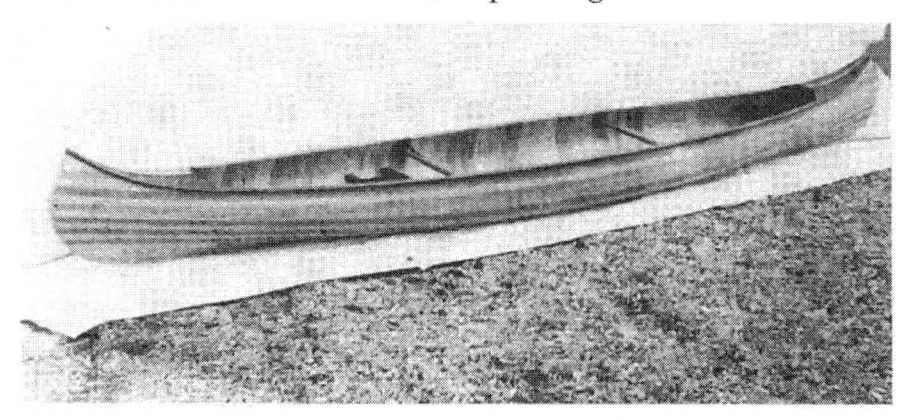

Mary Babare remembered that Day Islanders approved of Earl and Floyd and their proposed plans for a canoe factory. Records show that the brothers joined the Club in April 1921.

Floyd Willits at work.

Assisted by their father, Earl and Floyd built a modest house and a two-story framed building at the foot of the south spit hill. The building, their canoe factory, measured 26 feet by 65 feet. Windows lined the walls, inviting the sunlight to filter inside. Natural light was important during their early years on the Island as City Light's power ended on the south spit hill.[6] When needed, the brothers burned oil lamps. They powered their equipment with a gasoline motor.

Earl and Floyd partitioned the factory into four rooms. The parts-cutting room, where Earl worked, and the showroom took up the main floor. Drawers holding materials, patterns, and handwritten instruction books and ledgers covered the walls of the parts-cutting room. A yellow sheet of paper hung in the showroom where customers signed up to order a canoe.

The factory's second floor, Floyd's domain, housed the assembly room and finishing room. After Earl cut and stamped each piece of wood that went into a canoe, he grouped it according to wood tone and sent it up to Floyd. Floyd started the assembling process by softening the 4-inch inner planks in a steam box. Next, he clamped them over a jig. When dry, he transferred the planks to a solid mold, coated them with a marine glue, followed by a covering of muslin and more glue. The outer layer of 2-inch planks was placed on and fastened with 7,000 tiny copper nails.

The canoe was then fitted with thwarts and decks, gunwales were fastened and the wood finishing process began. Floyd filled the wood pores and sanded the surface. Next he placed the canoe in the finishing room and gave it four coats of varnish, which resulted in a finish that glowed like rubies.

A Willits canoe is 17-feet long, measures 34 inches across the beam, and has a depth amidships of 12 inches. A finished canoe weighs 75 pounds. Each canoe is identified by a numbered brass plate on the hull. [6]

In the early years on the Island, Earl and Floyd crossed the railroad tracks and searched the woods for clear, vertical-grain cedar. When they settled on a tree, they hired a feller to cut it down and haul it to a mill to be planed.

In later years they scouted for wood on the tideflats. Kay Williams, whose husband, George, ran St. Paul Tacoma's lumber yard, says, "They were the only ones that St. Paul allowed in to hand-pick individual pieces of lumber." The brothers used cedar for the hulls of their canoes, spruce for the seats and white oak for the stems. The keel was teak. Decks, thwarts and gunwales were either Honduras mahogany or teak.

The Willits brothers built their canoes during the warm weather months of the year. When the winter winds howled, Earl and Floyd pulled up near the wood stove and worked on canoe accessories. They designed a 48-square foot butterfly

Eva and Jesse Brown's daughter, Reba, on the beach by their Willits canoe. (Courtesy of Corinna Goff)

sail, rudders, fin keels, canvas covers and back rests.⁷

The brothers built over 900 what are now museum-quality canoes during the years they lived and worked on the Island. According to their record book, Jesse and Eva Brown were the first Islanders to buy a canoe after the factory opened on the south spit. They paid $103.50. Among other Islanders who owned Willits canoes were Fred and Connie Marvin, Les and Imo Sulgrove and Henry and Agnes Foss. The Fosses bought two of them. In 1939 they lent one of their canoes to two friends who retraced the (return) route of Lewis and Clark, continuing to the mouth of the Mississippi and New Orleans.⁸

Two of Earl and Floyd's customers, Jack and Sasha Calvin, accompanied by their dog, Kayo, paddled their canoe from Day Island to Juneau, Alaska. Calvin, who wrote an article for the *National Geographic Magazine* describing their 53-day adventure, praised the construction of their canoe. He wrote: "She was never manufactured, that canoe; she was created—created by two master craftsmen—built with the painstaking care that goes into a fine violin."⁹

The craftsmen were also dedicated to their community. Floyd accepted the office of Club president in 1926; Earl registered voters when Day Island became a precinct in 1928. They each served terms as secretary/treasurer of the Day Island Club. Floyd handled the job of water superintendent for 11 years. Earl acted as Day Island's "fire chief" in 1938.[10]

Both brothers married in later life. Floyd took Ruth Carter as his wife in 1939.[11] Earl lived with Floyd and Ruth until around 1944, when he married Laura Magill, a school teacher,[12] and moved into Tacoma. Eventually Earl divorced, Floyd's wife died, and the brothers ended up living out their days next door to the canoe factory. They died in the 1960s, about three years apart. By then Willits' canoes had gained world-wide recognition. One of the brothers' canoes can be seen at the Museum of History and Industry in Seattle,[13] another is on display at the Smithsonian Institute in Washington DC.[14] Earl and Floyd would be proud.

Almost Paradise
Chapter VI

Day Island greetings, Are greetings that make your heart glad....

"The '20s. Those were the days. After the remodeling of the club house, we Islanders entertained each other royally," recalled Mary Babare. "Back then living on Day Island was almost like living in paradise."

Late in 1921, Emil Loehrer, a carpenter, renovated the pump house creating one large room, which became known as the club house. Loehrer laid $209.98 worth of maple flooring and ran an exterior staircase down the south side of the

Day Island Clubhouse (Photo by author)

building to reach the postage-sized bathrooms tucked underneath the main floor. Ray Gillespie wired the building for electricity.[1]

The Islanders bought a $400 player piano from Sherman & Clay and formed a committee to promote social activities. The club house rented for $2.50 a night or $3.50 if the canvas that covered the floor needed to be taken up for dancing.[2]

Betty Wilcox, daughter of Sherman and Ethel Jonas, accompanied her family to the Saturday night dances when she was a little girl. She said it was a familiar sight to look in the corner and see a baby sleeping in a wicker chair oblivious to the sounds of music and laughter. She recalled that Gus Nyman always danced with her before her parents took her and her brother, Sherman ("Bud"), home to bed.[3]

Mary Babare said that a committee usually met together three or four times to plan a dance. They often asked

DING DONG BELL!!!

All ye good Citizens of Day Island Hearken:—

Ye are hereby summoned to assemble, in raiment glade, at Ye olde meeting house and partake of festivities and merriment on the night of

Friday, Aprile 1st

at the houre of nine o'clock

Ye olde time dances and melodies will reign supreme.

Come and bring All your Friends

DING DONG BELL!!!

Ed "Tige" Reynolds to illustrate the invitations and dance programs. Ed, a news cartoonist for *The Tacoma Daily Ledger*, liked to include the prancing little tiger cub, which dominated his cartoons, into a Day Island theme.[4]

Sometimes a dance began with a dinner or ended with late supper. Roy Norman favored the box socials, "when all the great Island cooks strived to outdo each other." At other times punch and cookies made up the bill of fare. Alcohol was not served in the club house. (However, Mary suspected that the men might have nipped a little when they checked on the children.)

Zelma Garvin wrote a Day Island song that was often sung at the dances. The words, which were sung to the refrain of, "Moonlight and Roses," are as follows:

> Day Island greetings
> Are greetings that make your heart glad,
> Day Island partings
> Are partings that make your heart sad.
> Sunset and gardens,
> Friends we have found loyal and true
> Day Island, we'll always be proud of you

Below is a "revised" version of Day Island's song as noted in a dinner program, November 9, 1929:

> Day Island meetings
> Are meetings that make your heart glad;
> Day Island partings
> Are partings that make your heart sad;
> Life's gay and happy,
> Just living the Day Island way,
> Friend-ly in all that we do or we say.

Connie (Titlow) Marvin[7] mentioned that the Day Island orchestra often played in the background while Day Islanders sang "their song." Members of the orchestra included Connie Marvin at the piano,[5] Earl Willits on drums, Walter Carlson[6] on the trombone, Roy Norman, saxophone, banjo,

Louie Bankhead,[7] and Oliver Craig,[8] who struggled with the French horn. "Oliver played off-key," laughed Connie. The orchestra rehearsed at the Marvin's house before a live performance.

Marion Van Winkle recalls that during her growing up years, the club house belonged to the young people on Friday nights. They had their own club, the junior Day Island club, and often held parties and dances. The girls had their choice of dancing partners as the boys outnumbered the girls three to one.

At age ten Marion (Dudley) Van Winkle,[9] originally from Yakima, moved to the Island with her parents, Virgil and Lillian Dudley, and eight-year-old brother, Bill. The Dudley family rented for two years and then built a single story house in the center of the Island where the park now stands.

"In the 1920s we rowed everywhere," recalled Marion. "My friend, Bess Tillotson, and I liked to row over to Fox Island for picnics.[10] One afternoon on the way home, a black fish swam under our boat, lifted us up on his back, then gently returned us to the water, and we continued on our way."

Virginia (Marvin) Tanzler remembers rowing ashore

Marion and Bill Dudley

at a deserted Fox Island farm. "There was a crumbling dock, its loose pilings covered with barnacles. This led to an old farmhouse which time and neglect had turned into a spooky, scary structure. Outside, there were apples, cherries and berries to pick, always plentiful enough to fill our buckets to overflowing."

"Often," wrote Virginia, "the trip home took longer than expected. Maybe we would have to make a detour because of whales spouting and rolling and adding adventure to the day. Or, strong tides might take us off course. If the captain was friendly, we might go aboard a tugboat to wait for the tide to turn."

Sometimes the children rowed over to McNeil Island and camped for three or four days. On one campout, while watching the inmates play baseball, the penitentiary guards rushed up and hastily escorted them off the Island. The young spectators later found out that Roy Gardener, notorious bandit and jailbreak artist, and two other prisoners had escaped. According to Paul Harvey's book, "Tacoma Headlines," Gardner's companions were shot to death, Gardner swam to Fox Island, stole a boat and escaped to the mainland. Sometime later, the police captured Gardner in Phoenix, Arizona.

(L. to r.) Mary Babare and Eva Brown reminisce in the '70s. (Photo by Paul Clee)

On Valentine's Day, in 1921, Marion's mother, Lillian hosted the first meeting of the Day Island Reading Club, which became a time-honored tradition. After hanging out the Monday wash, the women, armed with sandwiches and sewing baskets, gathered to read and listen to the latest book. Eva Brown remembered that Harriet Marvin, the club's first president, reviewed the first book. "We often stayed late to play a few hands of bridge. Unless it rained," laughed Eva. "Then we dashed home to grab the clothes off the line." The club invited all women on the Island to attend the weekly, noon day meetings. [11]

One Christmas Eve during the '20s, Lillian and Virgil Dudley, who sang soprano and bass, joined Gus Nyman, a tenor, and Agnes Foss, a contralto, for a harmonizing trek around the Island. Folks either flicked their porch lights in appreciation of the carolers' singing, or offered them sweet treats or a cup of cheer. "Mary Babare always presented them with a plate of freshly baked fattigmam," recalled Marion Van Winkle. The carolers and their neighbors looked forward to their annual Christmas eve celebration.

The Islanders sealed off their old well in the spring of 1923 and dug a new 480-foot deep artesian well that brought forth "the best tasting water in the country." Mary Babare recalled that folks from Tacoma brought a water jug when they came for a visit, to carry some good water back to the city. Connie Marvin thought that the water boosted the immune system. When illness confined her husband, Fred, to a hospital bed, Connie carried a jug of Day Island's water to his side. "The water brought him around in record time," exclaimed Connie.

Virginia (Marvin) Tanzler recalled that the new well sparked a celebration. "Everybody paraded around the Island, some beat on drums or pots and pans, others held up grey towels, labeled, "before," or clean, white towels labeled, "after." The *Ledger* reported that 200 Islanders participated in an impromptu, Sunday morning parade.[12]

The year 1923 brought two Scottish immigrants, Tom and Jeannie Mathie to Day Island. The Mathies with their daughters, Esther and Peggy, drove out from their north-end home in response to an ad which listed a summer cottage for sale on the west beach. They located the newly-built cottage out on the north sandspit, beyond the foot of the hill, where the pavement ended abruptly and a 450-foot wooden trestle began.[13]

The Mathies wandered through the one-bedroom cottage and discovered a fireplace in the living room, a kitchen, and a bath. A large porch faced the Olympics. The garage

A view of the north sandspit (Courtesy of Stan Marshall)

balancing on stilts, joined the wooden walk that ran from the back porch out to the trestle. The price was $4,500. "Mother and Dad didn't know if it was worth that," recalled Esther Mathie MacArthur. "It was tiny and without electricity."

The Mathies noticed the two other houses on the sandspit. Bob and Edna Merry's house stood next to the little summer cottage (1810 Day Island Blvd. W.). Bob was a foreman at Clear Fir Lumber Company. H. Eugene and Viva Emmons' house occupied a patch of land at the north end. Eugene Emmons owned and operated Tacoma Sash and Door Company.[14]

"As we investigated the neighboring houses and looked at the superb view, we noticed a man fishing in a rowboat, not far from shore. All at once he caught a huge salmon that sparkled in the sunlight," said Esther. "Daddy," the fisherman, exclaimed, "This is it! We'll take it. That began many happy years on the Island."

Tom installed electricity and helped Bob Merry haul gravel from the beach to fill in the low spots along the trestle. There was a need to build up the land as the water came up to the back door at high tide. Eventually the County filled in and built a road to the end of the sandspit.[15]

Tom and Jeannie allowed the owner of the Titlow Beach boat rental, to catch herring off their beach, which he sold for fishing bait. "He fastened a big net to the end of his old launch," recalled Esther. "His partner standing on the beach, held the other end of the net while the launch circled in a wide arc against the incoming tide and pulled their catch ashore." For the use of the beach, they sometimes gave the Mathies a dishpan full of fish. "Especially during the smelt run in September."

Over the years, Tom and Jeannie tired of shifting between two houses. They raised the cottage up off the beach, remodeled it, and moved in to spend their retirement years.[16]

Virginia Marvin atop the overhead bridge.

The Overhead Bridge

In 1924, the year after the Mathies purchased their summer house, Pierce County and the N.P. shared expenses and replaced the old Day Island bridge. The new $25,000 bridge spanned the railroad tracks, which eliminated the dangerous grade crossing.[17] Eva Brown recalled that the parents breathed easier when the children no longer needed to cross the railroad tracks to walk up to University Place Elementary School.[18] "We must have celebrated!" laughed Eva, "It was such a relief."

Opgenorth's Garden

In 1923, Mat and Irene Opgenorth bought a lot at 1950 Day Island Blvd. W. and built a small "temporary" cabin near the water's edge. Five years later, they added a two-story brick house to the property, where they raised their two sons, Bob and Charlie. The Opgenorths also purchased a lot in the center of the Island, near the club house, where Mat planted a vegetable garden. The garden, sometimes called, "the Pea patch," attracted more than birds; it became a neighborhood trysting place for the younger set, who roam-ed the Island at night.

For over three decades, as soon as the summer sun slid behind the Olympics, young feet

Mike and Pat Wilcox, 1944, in Henry and Agnes Foss' yard (Photo by Henry Foss)

turned toward the pea patch. "Night wanderings always ended up in the pea patch," recalled Pat Wilcox Flynn, a vegetable marauder from the '50s. "Freshly picked raspberries and peas made a perfect bedtime snack." (Pat received her first stolen kiss in amongst the raspberries.)

Back in the '20s, Pat's uncle, Sherman "Bud" Jonas, remembers stealing an ear of corn from Opgenorth's garden to make a corn cob pipe. "It led to many years of a bad habit," chuckled Bud.

Mat never attempted to keep the children out of the garden. Perhaps he grew a little extra to satisfy the appetites of the hungry night visitors.[19]

The South Sandspit

Frederick D. Dean, and his wife, Alice, built a summer home at the tip of the south sand-spit in 1925. The Dean's house, which perched on pilings in the lagoon, came about by happenstance.

Fred and Alice had been spending summers on the south sand-spit since around 1912, shortly after they moved to Tacoma from their native Texas. In the early days, they often camped out in one of Lemon's old boathouses. On one of their campouts, as Fred strolled along the skinny spit, he detected a hissing sound be-

Alice Dean displays her catch. (Courtesy of Pam Hubert)

neath the gravel and stooped down to investigate. He grabbed an old shingle and began shoveling down toward the sound, expecting to find gas. Instead he discovered water trapped in hardpan 18 inches beneath the surface of the gravel. Hardpan would anchor a building, reasoned Fred, and he promptly bought a pie-shaped lot "for a dollar a front foot,"

The Fred Dean house, 1938. (Courtesy of Pam Hubert)

A view from the south sandspit. Note the plank path. (Courtesy of Gunneld Willits)

and hired carpenters to construct a summer house, which Fred and their son, Fred Jr., enjoyed for many years. (The Deans became year-round residents in the 1950s.)

Following the Dean's lead, Oscar L. and Victoria Cayton built a house on a lot in the center of the sandspit. Their son, Forrest, mentioned that his dad was Pierce County Assessor for many years.[20]

Fremont "Goo" Cambell Jr. and his wife, Dora, built next door to the Cayton's place. Redheaded Fremont Cambell was Pierce County Auditor. The Cambell's had one son, Fremont III.

In 1926, the Cambells and the Caytons hooked up to Day Island's water. The Dean's water supply came from the A.P. Loomus property directly behind them, on the mainland.

Fred Dean enjoyed reminiscing about the early days. He recalled hiring a man named Larson to transport his

Duck hunters on the south spit. (Courtesy of Marion Todd)

family's goods to the bottom of the south spit hill. "Then I'd load everything into our boat from Larson's pony express wagon and row home. "I moved my son's harp in that manner," said Fred. Later a plank path ran the length of the sandspit, and Fred carted his belongings home in a wheelbarrow.[21]

Fred mentioned that deer used to swim over from Fox Island and wade ashore in his front yard before crossing the lagoon to the mainland. He also recalled that men used to fish at the bottom of the south spit hill. "From horseback, they threw out their nets and in no time dragged their catch ashore." Fred, a widower, lived on the Island until his death in 1977.[22]

The Garbage Brigade

In the 1920s, most of the Island's garbage ended up on the beach. Sometimes the tide failed to move it out fast enough, and it piled up along the water's edge and rotted. Mary Babare commented that although the health department frowned at the sanitary conditions on the Island, no changes occurred. "We were more concerned about the rubbish strewn along Sixth Avenue than our own problems," Mary remarked. "The west end of Sixth Avenue resembled the city dump. When the men on the Island failed to pressure city officials into cleaning up the unsightly mess, we women took matters into our own hands."

The women pulled on their gloves and went to work. For days they raked, shoveled and piled up tin cans, old stoves, beds, lanterns and barrels. Their labor paid off. The commissioner of Public Works (J.W. Silver) announced that the City would step in and finish the clean-up project.

"Our efforts helped for a while," chuckled Mary, "and a reporter rewarded us with an article and picture on the front page of the newspaper." The picture shows five of the women hard at work in their sturdy shoes, old dresses and hats. The caption reads: "Women of Day Island Manicure Sixth Avenue."[23] Among those photographed were Mary,

Grace Kepner, Flora Schriber, Connie Marvin and Lois Dille.

The Day Island Chapel

In 1927, the First Presbyterian Church started a number of mission Sunday schools in the outlying areas of Tacoma. One of them called, "the Day Island Chapel," met weekly at the club house.

Most of the neighborhood children enrolled in the Sunday school. Shirley Nyman Papé recalls that Lindsay Cambell, the stocky Sunday school superintendent, taught one of the classes. Cambell's daughter, Geraldine, played piano to accompany the singing. The average attendance was 22 for the year 1927, and the numbers increased over the years. Eva Brown said that the Sunday school offered a place where newcomers could get acquainted. The children looked forward to hearing Bible stories and singing praises to God.[24]

A "Dip" in the Bay

Montana native and labor attorney, Leslie Sulgrove and his vivacious wife, Imogene, moved to Day Island in 1927. They rented Burt Taylor's basement apartment (1930 Day Island Blvd. W.) for two years before purchasing a roomy two-story house which had a sun porch and a basement. They paid $8,200 for their home at 2228 Day Island Blvd. W.

Their daughter, Barrie, said, "My dad was an avid swimmer, and he and mother used to take a quick 'dip' in the Bay every summer morning before work, always every summer evening and on New Year's Day." Barrie recalls skinny dipping at night with her mother "to watch for the phosphorus." Imo, an award-winning stenographer, often worked with Les in his office at the Puget Sound Bank Building. She also served on the board of the Tacoma Day Nursery. Imo and Les loved to entertain, and they celebrated life on Day Island well into their 80s.[24]

Many friendships of all ages, that began in the '20s, blossomed over the years. Mary Babare said that those close-knit relationships contributed to a feeling of peace and unity that prevailed on the Island much of the time. Those who glance back agree. Back then, living on Day Island was almost like living in paradise.

Imo Sulgrove and her daughter, Barrie Sulgrove Smith, take a dip, 1947. (Courtesy of Barrie Smith)

Day Island, we'll always be proud of you.

Through Adventures and Trials
Chapter VII

In the 1930s, Day Island developed a plan to protect itsgrowing population from the threat of fire. The Day Island Club installed hydrants and built several small, wooden "houses" along the boulevards. Each structure, about the size of a dog house, held a thick fire hose. In the clubhouse, a cart outfitted with 500 feet of hose and two chemical extinguishers stood ready. Gus Nyman, the Island's fire chief, worked with a committee to oversee the plans and equipment.[1] Gus, also scout master of the newly-formed Day Island Sea Scout Unit 106, volunteered the services of his young charges in the fire prevention effort. The scouts never fought fires, but they did learn to wrestle the strong Puget Sound tides aboard their boat, the S.S. Pat.

Henry Foss, regional commander of the sea scouts, helped locate Pat, a government surplus naval shore boat for the 8-10 boys who comprised Unit 106. The scouts moored the 40-foot Pat in the lagoon behind the club house, where they held their meetings. Stan Marshall, a former skipper of Unit 106, recalls that they built a boathouse with lumber donated from Clear Fir Lumber Company. They also held dances to raise money to purchase a 25 horse-power motor for the S.S. Pat.

The scouts experienced many seafaring adventures. "Henry Foss called us when there was a log spill on the bay," reported Neut Grimes, "and we'd help bring the logs in." George Babare, Jr. remembers an outing when the scouts headed over to Fox Island in a small boat and got caught in a rip tide.

"Someone saw us struggling against the choppy water and called the Willits brothers, who came to our rescue." Ed Bradford remembered the summer Henry Foss let them use a 60-foot schooner, "Miss Tacoma." Ed fell overboard on one of the outings and almost drowned, but was pulled safely aboard. "A frightening experience," remarked Bessie Stephens, who was aboard to help husband, Frank, chaperone the scouts. "I will never forget it."

One of the scouts' adventures occurred off of Dash Point, enroute to Hood's Canal. The Pat collided with a whale and

Gus Nyman tackling a huge log on the Day Island beach while little Drew Foss observed circa 1920. (Courtesy of Shirley Papé)

slid up onto its large back. As the whale started to dive, it flipped its tail, which sent water flooding into the Pat's open hull. An article in *The Tacoma News Tribune* (1938) reported that the salty water bathed several scouts, but no one was injured, and the Pat and the whale parted company.

Unit 106 disbanded with the start of World War II. The "Pat" ended up tied to docks below Stadium High School, where she sank at her moorage.[2]

In 1934 my brother, Ken, a former Day Island Sea Scout, settled into a two-story house on the south spit with Lorayne, our sister, who was four years old, and our parents, Bill and Hazel Willoughby.

"We moved over from Browns Point in the dead of winter," said Ken. "It was so cold that Dad had to row under the house with a blow torch to thaw out the frozen water pipes."

My family in 1939. From l. to r. Lorayne, Bill, Marcia, Ken and Hazel.

Lorayne recalls the summer months when they made root beer. "We used to hang the bottles out the back window to cool them in the incoming tide."

Our parents, who had migrated from Saskatchewan following their marriage in 1923, felt uneasy living over water. Within the year, they moved up the hill to a two-story house with a deep porch and generous windows (2231 Day Island Blvd. W.). They leased for a year and then in 1936, a few years before my birth, purchased the house for $3,000.

Hazel, our petite mother, enjoyed growing and arranging flowers. In time Dad developed a green thumb. He began propagating rhododendrons, which in time filled the yard. The blooming evergreens spilled over into many of the neighbors' gardens, and into Day Island's mini park.

After Dad retired from his job as advertising manager for Foremost Dairies, he and Mother began spending part of the year in Palm Springs. Eventually they decided to relocate, and in 1972, my husband, Jerry Tucker, and I moved into my childhood home with our children, Steve and Sherry.

When my blue-eyed father looked back over his years on the Island, he liked to reflect on the lively dances at the clubhouse and good times with friends and neighbors. He also recalled when the mill burned and the neighbors crowded together on the east shore to view the spectacular sight.

Shortly after dinner on the 18th of October, 1934, fire erupted near the boiler room at Clear Fir Lumber Company. Flames spread rapidly, consuming the mill, shipping dock platform and 2,000,000 board feet of lumber. Before the fire department arrived, the fire buckled the company's steel railroad tracks and tossed piles of lumber through the burning platform into the water below. Flames shot skyward as the southwest wind pushed the showers of sparks and smoke toward the Narrows, steering them away from Day Island's bridge. The fireboat attacked the blaze at the north end of the plant, which saved the large planing mill.

The flames attempted to reach Day Island's bridge, but wind acted as a protective shield. That night only the telephone lines burned. The bridge survived.[3]

John Hanson's parents, Ed and Edna Hanson, bought a small two-story house next to the Sulgroves a few months after the mill burned. "They paid $8,500 for it," said John. "Dad thought that was an awful price." Ed, district claims agent for the Northern Pacific Railroad, came to Tacoma aboard the steamer, "Queen," in 1883.

After John graduated from dental school at the University of Southern California, he moved home with his parents and sister, Victoria. John joined the Army in 1942, and returned after the war. First he bought Gilbert Brown's small cottage (2224 Day Island Blvd. E.), then in 1949, he moved to 2218 Day Island Blvd. W., where he and his wife, Peggy, reside.

In the spring of 1935, Earl Brantner, a real estate salesman and musician, took a fateful stroll around Day Island with his blonde wife, Marion, and friends who were spending the summer on the south spit. The Brantners spotted a "for sale" sign on a cottage at 2214 Day Island Blvd. E. The young couple bought the cottage for $1,000. In 1947, three years after they adopted their son, Paul, the Brantners bought a larger two-story home at 2211 Day Island Blvd. W.

"Shortly after I moved to the Island, Doris Beattie knocked on my door and invited me to reading club," recalled Marion.[4] "Doris and I also attended rug club." Monthly, the women took turns opening their homes for lunch and an afternoon of braiding rugs.

After rug club on a windy afternoon in March 1937, chaos broke out on West Boulevard.

Wailing sirens pierced the air. With the north wind pressing against their backs, Doris and Marion hurried toward to the sirens and home. George Babare, Jr., returning from school, followed thick, heavy fire hoses that lay stretched out along the road. He wanted to see where they would end up. Moments before, Mary Babare had gone next door to the Norrisses to borrow something. As she chatted with her neighbors, she glanced out of the window, then shrieked in horror. Mary's house had burst into flames.

Day Island volunteers with their cart and hoses got there first. They fought a losing battle against the raging flames as the Tacoma Fire Department raced out from town. The fire spread rapidly, devouring the Babare's house and the contents.

Fueled by the north wind, the flames jumped over to Elmo Brown's little cottage, which the Norisses rented. Howard Norriss and Day Island volunteer firefighters were able to retrieve most of the Norriss' furniture before the fire swept through the house, leaving only the charred walls standing.

The *Ledger* reported that the Tacoma Fire Department

The Brantner home built at A. U. Mills. (Photo by author)

arrived in time to prevent the destruction of Rachel Gaucher's home, next to the little cottage, and Dr. James Carroll's home, to the north of Babare's. However, both homes were scorched. The Carroll's house was the worst, with about $200 in damages.

The Babare's fire, thought to be an electrical fire, sent the neighbors to their own homes for provisions. "They came running to our rescue," reported Mary. "Many brought blankets and coats, others came carrying food. Grace Kepner brought the best pork sandwiches I have ever tasted. With such kindness, we knew we would never want to live anywhere else," said Mary.

The Babares rebuilt after the fire. The Norrisses moved

to town. A lawn grew up where Elmo Brown's little cottage once stood. Within two years, the Carrolls replaced their scorched house with a two-story, $10,000 brick house. Only the smoke-filled memories of the fire lingered.[5]

In March, two years following the Babare's disaster, fire broke out at Lock McClean's house when a gas cooking system exploded and burst into flames. Day Island volunteers raced to the McClean's (2256 Day Island Blvd. W.) around 7 a.m. and battled the fire until the No. 9 hose wagon arrived from the city and helped extinguish it. Although water and smoke destroyed several hundred dollars worth of furniture and fixtures, the wooden house escaped damage, and Day Island volunteers rolled up their hoses and pulled their fire cart back to the clubhouse.[6]

As Clara and Lock McClean straightened up following their fire, flames of adventure were ready to ignite in the lagoon, behind the Ryan's house on East Boulevard. John and Maggie Ryan's teenage son, John Jr., and fellow Sea Scout Ed Bradford from University Place, were getting ready to shove off for Alaska in their leaky, lop-sided, home-crafted boat.

John and Ed's dream of adventures in Alaska began to smolder during their last year of high school. They hoped to live off the sea and the land—perhaps they'd stumble across some gold. All they needed was to find a boat to transport them to their land of opportunity.

Their search led them to the Hylebos Waterway on the tideflats, where they discovered a deserted hulk resting in the mud. The decrepit hulk belonged to Robert Dodd, the current commander of the Sea Scouts, and John and Ed bought it for $1 and towed it to the Ryan's house.

Over the next 16 months, the boys worked odd jobs and sank all their money into their boat. However, as John Ryan described in his book, "The Maggie Murphy," it was not money, but resourcefulness, that built the vessel. Whatever the "Maggie Murphy" gained, the neighborhood experienced a loss, including Clear Fir's Planing Mill.

Clear Fir transported unfinished boards from the mill to the door factory on a slow-moving rubber belt. The sight of clear-grained lumber parading by, proved too much for

Ed and John. They rowed across the lagoon, climbed up on the plank walk which ran adjacent to the belt, knocked off a few sheets of lumber into the mud below and hurried away. After dark, the boys rafted up the boards and towed them over to the Island. Like the mill workers, the Islanders were oblivious to their role in the "Maggie Murphy's" construction.

On the Island a neighbor began ripping apart an old motorboat about the time John and Ed needed a brass propeller shaft. The boys watched as he stripped off the brass fixtures and left them in a pile near the shore. After a two-week interlude, the young adventurers carried the shaft and bearings home to "Maggie." Another opportunity arose when John and Ed spotted a neighbor tearing down an old cabin. The boys helped themselves to the floor boards and the flooring became siding for "Maggie's" pilot house and 11-foot cabin. Both neighbors followed "Maggie's" progress, but neither seemed to recognize their individual contributions.

"Maggie Murphy," via the Inside Passage and powered with a 4-cylinder motor, gave the boys an adventuresome ride all the way to Ketchican. They fished together until the fall when John caught a steamer home to attend college.[7] He returned the following spring and fished aboard the "Maggie," while Ed joined the crew of a larger fishing vessel. John sold the boat at the end of the second season, but

The Maggie Murphy in the Day Island Lagoon, 1939 (Courtesy of John Hanson)

the "Maggie Murphy" fished on for 10 more years.[8]

My brother Ken recalls the spring he sent shivers of fear through his family. "I bought an old, weathered skiff from Gropper for $1, and patched up the holes in the bottom with sun-warmed tar from the road. During spring break from Stadium, Virgil Colgate and I hauled food, blankets and a 2 hp. Evenrude motor down to the boat and headed over to Anderson Island, accompanied by Skippy, my pint-sized dog. Toward dusk on the third day, a storm whipped up and soaked us so we started for home, around the west side of Fox Island. By then the boat was leaking like a sieve, and we took turns bailing. Somehow we got confused, missed Hale Passage and ended up in Purdy. We spotted an abandoned cabin, where we thought we could spend the night. We called our folks from a store, promising to be home in the morning. When we returned to the cabin, the woman next door noticed my sea scout uniform and thinking us trustworthy, invited us in. She fed us and fixed us a bed on the sun porch," said Ken.

"Morning came and went," recalled Ken. "After breakfast, we helped stack wood until the tide changed. As we came around Fox Island, we spotted Dad and the Willits brothers approaching in the Willits' beautiful launch. They witnessed what happened next. A tug passed us. It was pulling a barge, but I figured I could run across the cable before the barge got close. As I crossed the cable, the boat stopped dead in the water. We had run out of gas. Dad and the Willits brothers watched as I gassed up and got underway. We weren't in any danger, but the Coast Guard knew about our adventure and it made the newspaper.

"Mrs. Larson, the attendance clerk at Stadium, read about us in the paper and wasn't too hard on us when we reported to school a day late," said Ken. "Dad grounded me, and as I recall, that was the last I saw of the motor."

In the fall of 1939, native Tacoman, Melville Brown and his petite wife, Eunice, who hailed from Seattle, bought a two-story house south of John Ryan's house and next door to my family. "My grandmother, Murta Brown, noticed the 'for sale' sign while visiting across the street at the Gellermans

Mel and Eunice Brown's daughters Sara, Susan and Nancy in 1954. (Photo by author)

and instructed my parents to investigate," reported Susan Knight, the Brown's second daughter. Mel and Eunice inspected the house, purchased it for $4,000, and nested in. They stayed for the rest of their lives and raised three daughters, Nancy, Susan and Sara.[9]

Mel said that shortly after they bought their house, they noticed rats scurrying through their yard enroute to a feast of garbage on the west beach.

Ernie Felton eyed the littered beaches while unloading a cord of wood at the Schlarb's house on West Boulevard. (Ernie sold wood from Anderson Island for $4 a cord.) "When my husband saw trash on the beaches, he got the idea of starting a garbage pick-up service," recalled Felton's widow, Bertha (Honey) Kessler. "Felton asked John Schlarb, who was County commissioner, if he wanted to subscribe to a garbage service. Schlarb eagerly signed up." Honey canvassed the Island, searching for more subscribers. About a dozen families committed to the 50-cent-a-month service, but most continued to either throw their trash on the beach or hurl it out of the car window on their way across the bridge.

The Day Island Club scolded:

Garbage should not be thrown promiscuously on the beach only to be washed up on the next man's property. The practice of throwing garbage out of a car while crossing the Day Island Bridge is especially condemned as most of it hits the railing and stays on the bridge, and if it does reach the water, it floats around in the lagoon and is very objectionable. This is against a state law and anyone caught doing this will be prosecuted.

As Felton's garbage service grew, he expanded his route to include Titlow Beach and University Place. By then, World War II had opened up the job market, and Felton found full-time employment in the Bremerton Shipyards. Slim, petite Honey took over the garbage route.

"I remember the kindness and generosity of my customers," said Honey. "They often left me presents or cookies on top of the cans. Sometimes they carried their own cans to the side of the road, which helped. "However, before long," states Honey, "I developed a hernia from the lifting."

Honey hired Harvey Collins, a 16-year-old Bellarmine student to help with the route. "I drove the Chevy, and Harvey hauled the garbage and emptied it. We made a good team and picked up new customers," said Honey. "We stopped at nearly 300 houses before unloading at the City Dump on the tideflats which was free for commercial waste. "I liked Harvey. What a shock to learn that later on in life he murdered three people and ended up in Walla Walla where he was hanged."

After a few years, Honey tired of running the garbage

service and when Kordeil Larsen (founder of University Place Refuse Service) offered to take over the route, Honey gave it to him. By then, newspapers across the United States carried pictures of Honey and her garbage truck. Perhaps she was the first female garbage collector in the nation...at least she captured a first place in Day Island's history.[10]

Today, Honey might not recognize her old garbage route. Across the lagoon apartments and houses blanket much of the land. On the Island, which is now part of University Place, most of the original homes have been remodeled or replaced. There are more apartments, more people, more traffic than in years past. However, the fondness for the Island never changes. During long summer evenings, as fish jump and the sun slips behind the Olympics, Day Islanders pause, as in days past, to enjoy the beauty of the moment and to celebrate this place called home.

Day Island

A piece of land
small and thin
juts into Puget Sound.
Along its length
where sands begin
the crashing high waves pound.

They wash strong
on barricades—
some are swept to sea,
yet all the people
on the shore
live there most happily.

Behind is white-
crowned Mount Rainier,
in front the blue Cascades
and all about
swooping gulls
sing weird serenades.

They perch on tugs
that ride the tide;
Day Island people say
What fun to watch
where Salmon hide
and smiling children play.

—*Frances M. Johnson, February 1980*

Notes for Chapter I

1. For Wilkes chart of Day Island, see Chart of Admiralty Inlet, Puget Sound and Hood's Canal, Oregon Territory by the Exploring Expedition, 1841.

2. The journals of Joseph P. Sanford and Lt. George St. Clair, The Wilkes Expedition, May 15, 1841. File microcopies of Records in the National Archives: No. 75, Records of the U.S. Exploring Expedition under the command of Lieutenant Charles Wilkes, 1838-42, The National Archives, Washington, 1944.

3. Interview in 1975 with Frederick D. Dean, Day Island pioneer.

4. Charles Wilkes, Narrative of the United States Exploring Expedition, 1845, Vol. 1, p. xii.

5. Origin of Washington Geographic Names by E.S. Meany, p. 64.

6. T.T. Waterman, Manuscript of "Names of Places on the Southern Shore of the Sound From Johnson Point to the Vicinity of Tacoma."

7. T.T. Waterman, Indian notes and Monographs Miscellaneous Series No. 59, Notes on the Indians of Puget Sound, p. 67.

8. Marian Smith, The Puyallup-Nisqually, p. 263, Columbia University Press.

9. Article by Edward Huggins in the Seattle Times, March 9, 1852, "Perilous Trip with Food."

10. An unpublished manuscript by Nile Thompson, entitled, "a pre contract monograph of Steilacoom Indians."

Chapter I Notes...continued

11. Patent certificate No. 2531, Book 84, Deeds page 271.

12. Certificate No. 2531, Proof of right of pre-emption. April, 1970. A legal discription of the 160.70 acres is as follows: Lots numbered 1, 2, 3, and 6 and the Southeast of the Northeast of section 9; and the lot numbered 5 of section 4 in township 20 north of range 2 east. Warranty Deed. Book 3 Deeds, page 281. (Plummer's Atlas of Pierce County, Tacoma, 1889, shows Williamson's property.)

13. Ray Jordon,"Yarns of the Skagit County Ray's Writin's." 1974. Sedro Woolley, and "Chechacos All: the pioneering of Skagit," by the Skagit County Historical Society, pp. 69, 77, and 128.

14. Gary Fuller Reese, ea., Biographical sketch of August Valentine Kautz from, "Nothing Worthy of Note Transpired Today: The Northwest Journals of August V. Kautz," Tacoma Public Library, 1978.

15. Washington Historian, Washington State Historical Society, Vols. 1-2, p. 119.

16. Dixon H. Kautz, letter to father, George Kautz, May, 1896 and Dixon Kautz's journal in Kautz box #3, at the Washington State Historical Society.

17. Personal interviews in 1989 with Roy Norman, Harry Norman and James Reynolds about Dixon Kautz. Worthy Kanarr, the third property owner, tore down Kautz's cabin (1919 Day Island Blvd. E.) in 1953, when he cleared the land to build a two-story home and dug a swimming pool.

18. Kautz's ledger is at the Washington State Historical Society in Kautz box #3.

Chapter I Notes...continued

19. Mortgage the 160.70 acres for $10,000.00. Book 81 Mtgs. page 76. See satisfaction piece recorded in Book 138 page 571, Oct. 30, 1906. Also see partial satisfaction piece recorded in Book 135, page 137, April 23, 1906.

20. Telephone converations with Earl Mamlock, Stewart Nichols and Mel Monson, whose relatives considered buying Day Island.

21. Richard D. Osness, "Of Lions and Dreams, of Men and Realities: An Illustrated History of Fircrest, WA," 1976, p.5.

22. Hunt's History of Tacoma, Vol. III, p. 281-283, Eugene Church.

23. Personal interviews with children of Malcolm E. Gunston, Dudley Gunston and Grace Bates, 1980.

24. Interview with Anna Norris, Eugene Church's daughter, in 1982.

25. Articles of Incorporation of the Day Island Company, filed August 12, 1907, fee number 245964.

26. Warranty Deed, Book 319 Deeds, page 523. Eugene Church's, Day Island Company purchases Day Island.

27. Deed (tide lands) Fee no. 261695, Book 324 Deeds, p. 205.

28. Ad in the Tacoma Daily Ledger, Sept. 1, 1907, p. 20. "Elaborate Swiss Chalets to be built on Day Island by Prominent Men of Affairs."

29. Pierce County Commissioners Record Vol. 77, p. 500 (Permission to clear road around Day Island.)

Chapter I Notes...continued

30. Interview with Eva Brown concerning water system, 1976.

31. Tacoma Daily Ledger, August 30, 1908, p. 19. (advertisement)

32. An ad with a picture of the house that Church used as a real estate office, is in Tacoma Daily Ledger, June 16, 1912, p. 40. (1853 Day Island Blvd. W.) Ralph Woods purchased the home in 1910, according to Tacoma Title Company records.

33. Tacoma Title Co. Records. List of those who purchased lots from Day Island Company in 1908. (Block 2.) Willis Newton, F.W. Rudow, A.U. Mills, L.O. Janeck, J.W. Fiddes, William Gellerman, (2 lots) J.W. Rawlings, Daisy Weer and T.J. Cowell. (Block 3) G.W. Bullard, Mary Hayden, W.C. Scharf, Anita F. Wheeler, A.V. Love, J.J. Gross, Clara Murray, J.G. Newbegin, Chas. C. Jones, Linda C. Cone, J.P. Hovey, Katherine Patrick (2 lots), and Mary, Bertha, and Earl Moore (Block 4), John W. Moore (Block 7), Sam Butson (2 lots), Marie Gross, Dixon Kautz, Charles Forler and John Larson.

34. Charlie Forler. Interview with Charlie's niece, Marion Forler Todd. City Directory, 1932. (1923 Day Island Blvd. E.).

35. Fred and Eva Rudow, interviews with Mary Babare and Marion Van Winkle, Tacoma Title records, city directories. Rudow's house was at 2208 Day Island Blvd. W.

36. William and Stella Gellerman. Conversations with their children, Bill and Elizabeth Gellerman, City directories, Tacoma Title Co. records. The Gellermans lived at 2236 Day Island Blvd. W.

Notes on Chapter II

1. Sunday Daily Ledger, Aug. 18, 1912, p. 35, "Type of Attractive Bungalows Being Built on Day Island." (There is a picture of Tucker's house.)

2. Tacoma Title Company records, Tacoma City Directories for information on W.D. Tucker, who lived at 1849 Day Island Blvd. W. and Milo Stewart, who resided at 1933 Day Island Blvd. E.

3. Snyder Brothers mill and Clear Fir Lumber Company. City Directories, 1912-16. Tacoma News Tribune,"New Lumber Mill at Day Island." March 28, 1916, p. 35.

4. Information about the Stephens family and A. J. Littlejohn came from interviews with Frank and Bessie Stephens, their daughter, Miriam Kelso in the 1970s and 1980s, and from city directories. Stephens Grocery Store in Regents Park stood at the S.E. corner of Berkley and University Ave.

5. Rudolphus Weston. See W.P. Bonney's, History of Pierce County, Vol. II, pp. 960-61.

6. John Lemon, city directories, also see Tacoma News May 9, 1913, "Pioneer Citizen John J. Lemon is dead."

7. Northern Pacific Railroad and footbridge, 1914. Personal letter from H.G. Remus, director of valuation engineering, Burlington Northern Railroad, July 24, 1980 (description of footbridge).

8. Milk Route. Interviews with Myrtle Anderson, daughter of Nels and Ida Johansen, in 1976.

9. Interviews with Shirley Nyman Pape about her family, Tacoma City directories, records from Tacoma Title Company. The houses are at 1952 and 1954 Day Island Blvd. W.

Chapter II Notes...continued

10. Butcher boat. Interviews with George and Richard Uhlman, sons of Richard Uhlman, in 1976. Also interviews with Fred Dean. See article (with picture) in the Tacoma News Tribune, June 14, 1957.

11. Oscar Gustovensen. Conversations with Mary Babare, Henrietta "Tooty" Foss Hager, Gertrude Young of Fox Island, and Roy Norman. Roy's parents, Ben and Olga, bought Milo Stewart's home (1933 Day Island Blvd. E) in 1916, where they lived with Roy and his brother, Harry. They moved from Shelton when Ben found work yarding the logs aboard his tug, Petrel, for Clear Fir Lumber Company.

12. Yellowhammer Bus. interviews with Elmer Muzzy, 1976, also Eva Brown, Roy Norman, and Leonard Higgens.

13. See "Titlow's Dream," in the Tacoma News Tribune and Sunday Ledger, Oct 21, 1973, and article in the Tacoma Daily Ledger, December 30, 1910, p. 5, "Anxious to get that Road to Day Island."

14. Fred Gropper. Interviews with Frank Gropper, Mary Babare, Eva Brown, Helen Wick, Violet Smith. See article, TNT p. 1, by Don Duncan, "Day Island Squatter to Fool 'Em After All." December 17, 1954.

15. See an article in "The Fog Locker,"a Day Island Yacht Club publication, November, 1992, p. 4 entitled, "History of DIYC-1972,"narrated by Les McGaw.

Notes on Chapter III

1. Interviews with Eva Brown about Stromer and her family's early days on Day Island. The Browns built a small house at 2240 Day Island Blvd. W.

2. Naturalization papers no. 4172.

3. Olympic Leader (Port Angeles) July 2, 1915, p.1 "Tacoma to Port Angeles Two Hours by Hydroplane."

4. 1912 Tacoma city directory, p. 1063, lists Stromer's address at 6601 S. Lawrence St.

5. Tacoma Daily Ledger, April 27, 1914, p. 1, "Tacoma Aviator Undaunted by Fall."

6. Bomb dropping device—interview with Frank Stephens, also undated clipping, entitled, "New Bomb Dropper made by Aviator of Tacoma."

7. Conrad Hanson is mentioned in the undated clipping, "New Bomb Dropper made by Aviator of Tacoma." Myrtle Anderson, who delivered the milk to the Island, remembered Hanson and his connection with Stromer.

8. A description of Stromer's first Island built aeroplane, according to Frank Stephens. Also see Olympic Leader, p. 1, July 2, 1915, "Tacoma to Port Angeles Two Hours by Hydroplane."

9. Charles Roediger, article by Louise Hunt in The Tacoma News Tribune, Dec. 17, 1930, p. 2, "27 Years of Flying Noted."

10. Ione Titlow Wright. Interview, 1976.

11. The Tacoma Tribune, Feb. 20, 1915, p. 1 "Hydroplane Loses in Race with Auto," also The Tacoma Tribune,

Chapter III Notes...continued

    Feb. 21, 1915, "Maxwell Hangs Up Inter-city Record," p. 10. and Tacoma Daily Ledger, Feb. 21, 1915, p.3, "To Seattle in Just 27 Minutes," and The Tacoma Daily News, Feb. 20, 1915, p. 1 "Airship Sales from Tacoma to Seattle." See also, The Seattle Post Intelligencer, Feb. 21, 1915, p. 1, "She Flies Here From Tacoma."

12. Twelve-seat plane. Interview with Frank Stephens and article in the Astoria Evening Budget, March 2, 1916, "Plans Air Service, Tacoma."

13. Article about Hallin in Washington Ochdeffsvenska Befolknina, by Ernst Skarstedt, p. 361, Washington Printing Company, 1908.

14. Interview with F. Bernard Wright, 1976, about Hallin. Bruce Johnson mentions Hallin in his article, "Waterborn Workers From a Bygone Era," The Tacoma News Tribune, May 16, 1976.

15. The Hallins built at 1905 Day Island Blvd. E.

16. Louise and Louis Brown, interview with Louise, 1976. The Browns rented at 1937 Day Island Blvd. E. before building a home at 1943 Day Island Blvd. W. They had one daughter, Shirley.

17. Carl Hallin's obituary notice, Tacoma News Tribune, January 18, 1944, p. 6.

18. Jack and Eva Heuertz's daughter, Mona Mae Huertz, married my brother, Ken Willoughby, in 1948.

Notes on Chapter IV

1. Tacoma Daily Ledger, Jan.9, 1916, "Day Islanders Must Pay or Lose Light," p. 4.

2. Officers of the Day Island Club. See Bylaws of the Day Island Club, Article II.

3. A.U. Mills. See W.P. Bonney's History of Pierce County, Vol. I, p. 589, and article on Mills in The Tacoma Daily Ledger, August 20, 1928, p. 1 "Former Official Called By Death." For interesting reading on Mills and his involvement during the expulsion of Chinese in Tacoma in 1885, see Bonney's History of Pierce County, Vol. 1, pp. 463, 469 and 479.

4. Jim and Zelma Garvin. Conversation with Gertrude Bonnell, sister of Zelma Garvin, Tacoma Title Company Records and Tacoma city directories. Address: 1904 Day Island Blvd. W.

5. O. Ben Olson (Marie.) W.P. Bonney's History of Pierce County, Vol. III, p. 370, Tacoma Title Company Records and Tacoma city directories.

6. Day Island Club certificate of Incorporation, Article 37925, Sept. 7, 1915.

7. Pierce County Commissioners report on the history of the Day Island Bridge by Robert A. Jacques, chief civil deputy, entitled, "History of construction, maintenance and re-construction of Day Island Bridge," March 16, 1955.

8. Day Island's flag. See Day Island Club minutes, Vol. 1, p 25.

9. Records show that Dr. J.R. Fisher charged a $10 annual fee per lot for water from his property.

Chapter IV Notes...continued

10. Permission to dig well. See Day Island Club minutes, Vol. 1, p. 31, Jan. 24, 1918, and Pierce County records, Vol. 35, p. 611, case 730.

11. Church sells pipeline. See Day Island Club minutes, Vol. 1, pp. 35 and 39.

12. Bids for well. See Day Island Club minutes, Vol. 1, p. 31.

13. Day Island Club minutes for Sept. 12, 1918 mention that an engraved plate with the names of the water committee be made and placed at the entrance of the club rooms.

14. George and Harriet Marvin. Letters from their daughter, Virginia Tanzler.

15. Henry and Agnes Foss. Interviews with the Fosses and their daughter, Henrietta "Tooty" Hager in the 1970s. See Day Island Club minutes, Vol. 1, 63, and Tacoma Daily News, June 30, 1914, "Hanson-Foss wedding." Foss Tug and Launch Company began modestly in 1890 when Henry's mother, Thea, began buying and renting out rowboats. Henry's father, Andrew, later added towboats and launches to the fleet. The company was reorganized and renamed in 1914, the year Henry and Agnes married.

16. George and Mary Babare. Interviews with Mary Babare, also see articles in History of Pierce County, Wa., Taylor Publishing Co. Dallas, Texas, 1990. "On the Waterfront, p. 8, and "Stefan and Lacretia Babare," p. 277, by Mary (Babare) Love. An article in the Tacoma Daily Ledger, April 18, 1920, p. B5, "North End Homes Have New Owners mentions the Mills house sold for $3,500. Flag pole moved. See Day island Club minutes, Vol. 1

Chapter IV Notes...continued

17. Interview with Roy and Harry Norman in the 1980s about the day and year Day Island's roads were paved. Also see Pierce County records, Vol. 37, p. 359, "Regents Park Day Island Blvd. Road," May 8, 1920.

Notes on Chapter V

1. Article by B.W. Brinthall in The Tacoma News Tribune, Aug. 19, 1939, "Their Canoes are Known World Wide."

2. Interview with Gunneld Willits, widow of Earl and Floyd's half-brother, Leonard Willits.

3. Tacoma City Directories, 1908-10.

4. The Daily Ledger, Tacoma, Wash., June 21, 1914, p. 1, "Tacoma High School Boys As Pioneers of Industry."

5. The Tacoma News Tribune Sunday Ledger, July 18, 1965. p. A 14, "Day Island is 'World Apart' from the Mainland."

6. Willits Brothers brochure.

7. Article by Holly Hughes in Wooden Boat, Nov./Dec. 1983 issue, pp. 82-86, "The Willits Brothers Canoes."

8. An interview with Earl and Floyd in the 1950s.

9. An article in the National Geographic, Vol. LXIV, No. 1, July 1933, by Jack Calvin, "Nakwasina" goes North.

10. The Day Island Club minutes show the club activities of the Willits brothers.

11. An article in the Tacoma News Tribune, April 30, 1939, p. 6-B. "Home on Day Island: Miss Carter Becomes the Bride of F.C. Willits."

12. Laura Magill Smith Willits. An obituary notice in the Tacoma Morning Tribune, Jan. 18, 1994.

13. Marine Digest, Vol. 46, May 18, 1968, p. 16, "Historic Sailing Canoe Presented Museum."

Chapter V Notes.....continued

14. Murray Morgan's article in The Morning News Tribune, Nov. 1, 1990, p. 7, "Willits Brothers Crafted Perfection into a Canoe," notes that a Willits canoe is displayed at the Smithsonian.

Notes on Chapter VI

1. Ray and Anna Gillespie (children, Gordon & Elizabeth) built at 2244 Day Island Blvd. W. Ray owned R.S. Gillespie Electric Supply Company.

2. Remodeling the club house, see Day Island club minutes, Vol. 1 and record book, Vol. 1.

3. Sherman and Ethel Jonas rented the Warren house at 1920 Day Island Blvd. W. Sherman worked at F.C. Jonas & Son Hardware on 6th Avenue. Their daughter, Betty, married Horton Wilcox and moved back to Day Island with their children Mike and Pat in 1942. Their third child, Ted, was born in 1951. The Wilcoxes moved to Seattle in 1955.

4. Mary and Ed Reynolds built a house in 1921 at 2228 Day Island Blvd. E., where they lived with their son and daughter until moving to Portland in 1924. See clipping file, Tacoma Public Library.

5. Fred and Connie (Titlow) Marvin lived at 2204 Day Island Blvd. W. Fred, brother of George Marvin, developed the Merchants Transportation Company and was president of the Tacoma Port Commission, Tacoma News Tribune, p. 1, March, 1951.

6. Walter and Ethel Carlson lived at 1912 Day Island Blvd. W.

7. Louie Bankhead, son of William and Blanche Bankhead and his brothers, Cecil and Ted, lived at 2209 Day Island Blvd. E. William was an engineer at Clear Fir Lumber Co.

8. Oliver and Josephine Craig, 2201 Day Island Blvd. W. Oliver owned Craig Furniture Company at 1137 Broadway, Tacoma. Jo married William "Jack" Welch after Oliver died.

Chapter VI Notes...continued

9. In 1929, Marion Van Winkle married Ken Panchot who hailed from St. Paul. The couple met in Yakima. In 1938 they moved to Day Island with their son, Dudley. In 1941, they built a house at 1937 Day Island Blvd. W. Two years later, Ken, who worked for Puget Power, died of a heart attack while camping with his family at Mt. Rainier. In 1948, Marion married Edgar "Rip" Van Winkle. Widowed a second time, Marion lived in her home until her death in 1996 at age 86.

10. Bess Tillotson lived at 1916 Day Island Blvd. W. with brother, Harry Jr. and sisters, Helen and Mary, and parents, Harry and Lillian.

11. The reading club, which evolved into a luncheon club, continues to meet several times a year.

12. Article, "Day Island has Celebration for Well Completion," Tacoma Daily Ledger, May 14, 1923, p. 3.

13. Most likely Realtor G.D. Grant built the trestle. An ad in the Ledger, March 28, 1915, notes his plans to extend the Blvd.

14. In a phone interview in 1976, Eugene Emmons mentioned that he, Viva, and daughters, Susan, Eleanor, Helen and Joan, spent summers at 1804 Day Island Blvd. W. from 1918-28. Viva, a teacher/author, wrote, "Roots of Peace," and "India in Transition."

15. Pierce County appropriated funds for a north end road Jan. 20, 1928.

16. The Mathies' daughter, Esther, with her husband, Donald MacArthur and children, Donald Jr., and Marian, moved in the basement apartment to care for the Mathies in their old age. The MacArthurs later moved into an apartment on East Blvd.

Chapter VI Notes...continued

17. Article on the new bridge, "County and NP to build Viaduct." Tacoma Daily Ledger, Jan. 19, 1924.

18. In 1927, University Place School's new Principal, George Curtis, rented a house on East Blvd. They lived on the Island for several years.

19. Opgenorth's garden was at 2204 E. Blvd. Bob Opgenorth's daughter, Mary Mangold, resides in the home with husband, Audi, and sons, Drew and Evan.

20. Interviews with Forrest Cayton about his family, the Cambells and the south spit.

21. Pierce County records for Nov. 26, 1929, show that funds were budgeted for Day Island bulkhead beach road to be done early in 1930.

22. Interviews with Frederick Dean in the 1970s.

23. Article in the Tacoma Daily Ledger, April 30, 1926, p.1. "Women of Day Island Manicure Sixth Avenue."

24. In time, most of the children attending the Sunday school lived off the Island, and their going and coming created traffic problems. In 1937 the Sunday school relocated to the abandoned "Narrows" tomato warehouse on Grandview near W. 27th Street. In 1941 the Sunday school moved into University Place School. In 1943, the Sunday school reorganized and became University Place Presbyterian Church.

25. During their retirement years, the Sulgroves built a smaller house next door (2220 Day Island Blvd W.) Their daughter, Barrie, and her husband, John Smith, moved into the large house where they raised their two daughters, Jody and Melnee.

Notes on Chapter VII

1. Fire prevention. Interview with Mary Babare, and Day Island Club minutes.

2. Sea Scouts. Interviews with former sea scouts, Ed Bradford, John O'Ryan, Stan Marshall, nephew of Edna and Bob Merry, Neuton Grimes, son of Ben and Edna (1805 Day Island Blvd. W.), Julian Whaley, son of Dr. Estelle and Jacob Whaley. Jacob, was superintendent of sawmill section at Clear Fir.) (1904 Day Island Blvd. W.) I interviewed Renee Paine, sea scout historian. See Tacoma News Tribune article, July 11, 1938, "Sea Scout Ship and Whale Collide."

3. Clear Fir fire. Tacoma Daily Ledger article, Oct. 19, 1934, p. 1 "Plant Loss Estimated at $300,000." Tacoma News Tribune article Oct. 19, 1934, p. 1 "$300,000 Fire in Mill." See also "100 years of fire fighting in the city of destiny, Tacoma, WA," by Clyde Talbot and Ralph Decker, ed. Ann Roush. Pyro Press, copyright 1981. (The door factory, south of the bridge, burned down May 26, 1942.)

4. Doris and Stan Beattie moved permanently to Day Island (2243 Day Island Blvd. W.) following their marriage in 1934. Doris met Stan in a bookkeeping class at Stadium High School. The Beatties had two daughters, Gwen and Janice.

5. Babare fire. Tacoma Daily Ledger, March 25, 1937, p.1 "Flames Threaten Day Island," Tacoma News Tribune March 25, 1919, p. 8, "Day Island Homes Burn."

6. McLean's fire. Tacoma News Tribune, March 25, 1938, "Explosion Starts Fire on Day Island."

7. The Maggie Murphy. Interviews with Ed Bradford and John O'Ryan in the 1980s. See the book the "Maggie

Chapter VII Notes...continued

Murphy," copyright, 1951, W.W. Norton and Company, Inc. During the '30s the O'Ryans lived at 2215 Day Island Blvd. E.

8. See article by John O'Ryan in the Seattle Post Intelligencer, Dec. 7, 1978, p. A18, "Still Hooked on the Maggie Murphy." Newspaper reporter John Ryan added an "O" to his name in the 1970s.

9. Nancy Brown and Susan Knight still enjoy living in their childhood home, where Susan raised her son, Rick.

10. The garbage lady. Interview with Bertha (Honey) Kesler. Also, newspaper clippings from approximately 1942.

Made in the USA
San Bernardino, CA
07 February 2019